D1426658

SACRAMENTO PUBLIC LIBRARY

3 3029 00829 5719

3t   BIRMINGHAM
G4
19   Information Services

CARMICHAEL

L LIBRARY
AVENUE
RMICHAEL, CA 95608

07-01

WITHDRAWN FROM COLLECTION OF
SACRAMENTO PUBLIC LIBRARY

	DATE		

JUL   1983

OCT 8 2

© THE BAKER & TAYLOR CO.

JUL   1986

LOVE
CANAL

LOVE
CANAL

MY STORY

LOIS MARIE GIBBS

**as told to
Murray Levine**

STATE UNIVERSITY OF NEW YORK PRESS
Albany

Published by
State University of New York Press, Albany

© Lois Gibbs and Murray Levine, 1982

All rights reserved

Printed in the United States of America

No part of this book may be used or reproduced
in any manner whatsoever without written premission
except in the case of brief quotations embodied in
critical articles and reviews.

For information, address State University of New York
Press, State University Plaza, Albany, N.Y., 12246

Library of Congress Cataloging in Publication Data

Gibbs, Lois Marie
    Love Canal.

    1. Love Canal Chemical Waste Land fill (Niagara
Falls, N.Y.) I. Levine, Murray, 1928-
II. Title.
TD181.N72N513   363.7'28   81-14508
ISBN 0-87395-587-0   AACR2
ISBN 0-87395-588-9 (pbk.)

CARMICHAEL

c.2

To All
Who Have Suffered
and
To All
Who Have Helped
at Love Canal

CONTENTS

ACKNOWLEDGMENTS

Patricia Ann Conn, my mother, is the most precious person in my life. Without her, I would not have been able to take on the "fight" at Love Canal. She not only provided me with support and encouragement but also gave my family the love and care they needed in my absence.

Ken and Bev Paigen—a family that unselfishly sacrificed three years of their lives to assist the people at Love Canal—will always have a special place in my heart. Beverly, a great scientist, had the courage to "stick her neck out" regardless of the personal costs to help resolve the canal problems. Ken and Beverly are two people that I respect as scientists and truly admire as "caring" people. I would also like to extend a special thanks to the Paigen children for allowing us so much of their parents' time.

Wayne and Kathy Hadley are more than a sister and brother-in-law to me. I will always remember them as the "teachers." They were both there at the start of Love Canal to help me found our organization, teach me politics, science, pubic speaking, and more. I will always be eternally grateful for the help and guidance they gave me to fight this awesome battle. Without Wayne and Kathy, I may have never gotten involved.

Richard Lippes has given me support and guidance throughout our fight for which I will always be thankful. As our attorney, he represented us many times, without concern for fees, but rather with a concern for people. Besides this role as our attorney, I also respect and admire him as a caring person.

Stephen Lester is a person I respect as a scientist and admire as a person. Although he played a fence-sitting role at Love Canal, he was still able to provide us with the professional guidance and understanding we needed to solve the canal problems.

Murray and Addie Levine are two people that have given their "all" to the canal crisis. They have helped me in many ways from cutting newspaper articles to writing this book. I will always be grateful to both of them for their support, encouragement, and the love they have given me during the past three years.

Debbie and Norman Cerrillo were there at the start of Love Canal and never gave up, even though they were moved out of the neighborhood in 1978. They both sincerely cared about their suffering neighbors that were left behind. I will always be very grateful to the Cerrillo family for hanging in there and giving of themselves to help others. We could not have asked for a better vice president than Debbie.

Luella and Norman Kenny will always have my admiration for their courage, support, and work at Love Canal. The Kenny family lost someone very dear to them, but instead of hiding, they took a stand to fight for the other children of Love Canal. Jon Kenny, their seven-year-old child, lost his life to the Love Canal chemicals.

John and Grace McCoulf and Maude have my thanks for the time they sacrificed to work at Love Canal on typing, fund raising, day care, and numerous other things they helped me with during the crisis.

Marie and Ed Pozniak are one canal family I truly love and admire. They sacrificed three years of their lives to work in the office every day, patiently anwering phone calls from residents with problems, complaints, and fears and working into the early hours of the morning to complete a survey. They never missed a meeting, protest, or complained about attending. There are no words that could even begin to express the admiration and gratitude that I feel for this family. They are truly very special people.

Barb and Jim Quimby are the people who had it "all" and survived. I would like to extend a special thanks to them for all their help, especially with EPA and support throughout the canal crisis.

Phyllis and Len Whitenight are appreciated for all their help, support, and encouragement they gave me throughout the canal crisis.

Jo Ann and Bob Kott, for their help in the past and for their continuing efforts at Love Canal, I give special thanks.

I would like to extend a special thank you to the following families, as well as the many other families at Love Canal and across the nation. Without the support of these people, the Love Canal crisis may have been completely ignored.

Jan and Dave Alexander
Kathy and Raymond Aul
James Ball and family
John Ball and family
Stephen Barron, M.D.
Thomas Bartosiewicz, Senator
Margaret Bates and family
Anthony Bax (Tops)
Carolyn and Lewis Blevins
Frank Budway (Super Duper)
Allen and Sophie Casler
Harvey Cohen (Mc Donalds)
Bill Daly (Super Duper)
John Daly, Senator
Joseph and Sharon Dunmire
Arthur and Catherine Eberhart
Environmental Defense Fund
Linda and William Foy
Patricia and Ernest Grenzy
Jo Ann and Gary Hale
Lucy Hanrahn and family
Jean and Gerald Hasley
Hepburn family
Iadicicco family
Jacoby family
Jacob Javits, Senator
William Jusko, Ph.D.
Kalano family
Charles Keith and family
Konecki family
Bob and Florence Krul

Ralph Kusner (Super Duper)
John LaFalce, Congressman
Ray and Louise Lewellen
Licht family
Lee and Lila Lutz
Mervack family
Walter Mikula
Shirley Mort
Daniel Moynihan, Senator
Matthew Murphy, Assemblyman
David Nathan
Nowak family
Lee and Don Nugent
Pivka family
Pries family
Elizabeth and Joseph Retton
Rizzo family
Michael Sado, M.D.
Patricia and Raymond Sandonato
Reverend Sterns
Lynn and Harry Tolli
Tracy family
William Waggoner
Walker families
Zimmerman family
Unions: Abrasive Workers,
    Local 8-12058; United Auto
    Workers Locals 508, 634,
    686, 846, 1173, 774, and 501
Western New York Cap CAP
    Council.

INTRODUCTION

Lois Gibbs once characterized herself as the housewife who went to Washington. In that description lies much of her story. She is a housewife, and she went to Washington. She is also a mother defending her home and her children. Her home and her children were threatened by a forgotten, but leaking, toxic chemical dump site, the now infamous Love Canal, located near her home in Niagara Falls, New York. Love Canal is now a symbol known worldwide, a synonym for environmental pollutants of all kinds, the effluvia of an advanced industrial and technological machine that has created hitherto undreamed-of marvels and wealth, but which now, paradoxically, threatens our very existence.

There are three reasons for telling Lois Gibbs's story. First, it is an inspiring story of an attractive young woman who, by outward appearances, might be just the person one would select in a search for the typical American woman. At the time this story began, she was twenty-seven years old, white, Protestant, married with two children. Both she and her husband Harry, a chemical worker, have high school educations. They owned their own home, a modest, three-bedroom bungalow with a basement they finished themselves, located in a quiet, residential neighborhood in a small upstate city. Their house and their street could be the set for a movie about the typical American family. Harry and Lois worked to save for the down payment for their home. When their children were born, Lois stopped working and stayed home, cooking, cleaning, gardening, and sewing. Women's liberation was a subject for raucous humor among her friends. Neither she nor Harry was involved in community organizations; nor did either have more than a passing interest in politics. Lois Gibbs—in many ways a private, inward person—thought of herself as being painfully shy.

Yet in the midst of turmoil, she organized a neighborhood association, was elected its president, and, in short order, learned to face down governors, senators, and mayors and to deal with bureaucrats, scientists, professors, lawyers, and the national media. From a woman who had skipped a day of school when she had to present a book report, Lois became the spokeswoman and political strategist for a thousand families in Niagara Falls. She conducted meetings, gave press conferences, confronted officials, negotiated with the governor and his representatives, appeared on national television, testified before Congress, addressed college classes, and was recognized by the President of the United States for her efforts. She learned about law, politics, toxicology, and engineering and, in the process became something of a natural epidemiologist.

Lois Gibbs's story deserves to be told—not just because she was (and is) courageous, but because hers is an inspiring story of a seemingly ordinary woman who, in response to crisis and challenge, transcended herself and became far more than she had been. That process is still going on.

That Lois Gibbs went to Washington was no accident. The second reason for telling her story is that it adds to our knowledge of the relationship between citizens and their government and of the relationship between experts—genuine or would-be—and those whose lives are influenced by their decisions. Government officials and their coteries of experts are supposed to serve citizen-taxpayers, but they do not always do this, or do it well. Ordinary citizens cannot trust officials and/or experts to always act in their best interests. As she became more and more involved, Lois Gibbs became convinced that citizens must be heard, and that, to be heard, both she and those she represented would have to demand a hearing.

She was moved to organize her neighborhood after a school official told her there was no evidence of danger to her child in attending the 99th Street School, even though the school was located on top of Love Canal while newspapers and public health officials were trumpeting the danger. Her six-year-old son developed asthma and seizures, both common reactions to toxic chemicals, after he started attending the 99th Street School. She thought at first that he was merely a sickly child; then she became convinced that his illnesses were the result of exposure to toxic chemicals and, armed with a letter from her physician, she tried to have him transferred to another school. School officials denied the request, telling her there was no evidence of danger, and thus no reason to close the school.

It was this denial that convinced Lois Gibbs the only way she could make herself heard was through a community-wide effort. It was then that she began going from house to house, talking to neighbors and hearing about their many health problems. While public health officials claimed that prolonged studies were needed, Lois, on the basis of conversations with her neighbors, *in their own homes*, came to believe that the canal was a disaster area. She learned, however, that public officials view problems and define issues from their own perspectives, which are not necessarily the perspectives of the people immediately affected by their actions and decisions. At meetings with citizens, public officials and experts tell, inform, and sometimes conceal; they do not consult. With all of their resources, officials can make decisions—especially decisions with political overtones—that are, on their face, absurd and run contrary to all common sense. If Love Canal has taught Lois Gibbs—and the rest of us—anything, it is that ordinary people become very smart very quickly when their lives are threatened. They become adept at detecting absurdity, even when it is concealed in bureaucratese and scientific jargon. Lois Gibbs learned that one cannot always rely on government to act in the best interests of ordinary citizens—at least, not without considerable prodding. She determined that she would prod them until her objectives were attained. She led one of the most successful, single-purpose grass-roots efforts of our time. The Love Canal Homeowners Association (LCHA) has attained its goal of permanent relocation for all affected residents of Love Canal who wished to move. Because she, the other residents, and the members of the LCHA fought hard, they made front-page news, eventually pressuring New York State and the federal government to take action and relocate those residents.

Beyond achieving their own salvation, though, residents of Love Canal, through their efforts, have influenced national policy. They have aroused the nation's consciousness to the danger of toxic wastes. The United States Congress has enacted legislation to clean up abandoned toxic waste dumps, in hopes of preventing future Love Canals. The New York State legislature, and the legislatures of other states as well, are considering ways of coping with and preventing similar tragedies. The Love Canal home-owners have alerted other communities to the dangers. In some instances, they have been instrumental in helping communities resist placement of toxic dumps, even supposedly safe ones, next to their schools or near their water supplies. In the fight for her home and children, Lois Gibbs was fighting for the safety and health of millions of other homes and families. Her story should be told because, in relating the story of her personal fight, Lois can instruct the rest of us about fundamental issues and problems that arise in the relationship between citizens and government, between citizens and experts, and between citizens and corporations.

There is, however, a third reason for Lois Gibbs telling her story: the story of the inner meanings and feelings of *humans*, a story told from the perspective of one human being, provides a necessary and powerful antidote to the moral illness of those cynics and their professional robots who speak the *inhuman* language of benefit-cost ratios, who speak of the threat of congenital deformities or cancers as acceptable risks. The dollar cost of disposing of toxic wastes, the local cost of regulating industry, and the probability that an industry will be driven away to spread poison in a more amenable part of the country—all can be argued abstractly. One might speak of dollars per ton of waste, of additions to the cost of living index, of the number of jobs lost, and of the rate per hundred thousand of liver cancer, and consider the issues dispassionately. But governors and legislators, industry executives, economists, and health commissioners do not usually live on top of toxic waste dumps. They are seldom awakened in the middle of the night by a phone call from a pregnant woman suddenly panicked because her unborn child has stopped kicking, fearful that it may have died in her womb or that it will be born deformed. They don't see the heartbreak on the face of a mother who has lost her seven-year-old son to nephrosis. They don't have to live with the thought that the leukemia which took a child ten years ago was not an unfathomable act of God but the result of human carelessness, of greed or stupidity, or, worst of all, that the disease might have been avoided. They don't have to deal with the irrational, but nevertheless real, guilt of fathers and mothers who feel that it was somehow their fault that they purchased property dangerous to their children and are now trapped, unable to leave without bankrupting themselves. They don't have to take coffee with the depressed couple near retirement who had dreamed of selling their house and moving to a warmer climate or to be near friends or children in another part of the country, and who now find their property worthless because no one will buy it. The bureaucrats and the economists, the toxicologists extrapolating from the unknown to the unknowable, the public relations people trying to put the best face on corporate crime or governmental ineptitude or simply the crass politics of expediency, the flak-catchers who twist and squirm when confronted at public meetings but who later comfort themselves with half a bottle of Scotch—none of these are haunted by the thought that even if *they* are safe, their children's unborn children may suffer.

Lois Gibbs lives with these fears. Some are her own and some are those of her friends and neighbors who rely on her for strength. They call her, often late at night, to share their fears and obtain some hope when helplessness, fear, or rage makes sleep impossible. It was the stoicism of these friends and neighbors in the face of personal tragedies—cancers, deformed children, miscarriages, nervous disorders, suicides, asthma, and epilepsy—that moved Lois Gibbs to organize her neighbors. It is her own suffering and her knowledge of their suffering that help her keep fighting. It is their suffering and their strength that make Love Canal not a story of dollars, logistics, statistics, tables of numbers, and lists of unpronounceable polysyllabic organic compounds; rather, it is the story of individuals and families, of feelings and meanings. Hers is a story that needs to be told if we are to comprehend the true *human* significance of environmental pollution.

Murray Levine
Director, Clinical/Community Psychology Program
SUNY at Buffalo

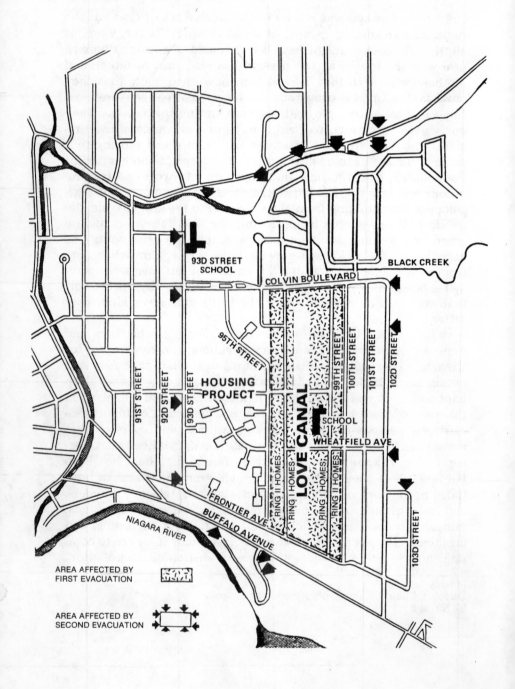

93D STREET
SCHOOL

BLACK CREEK

COLVIN BOULEVARD

95TH STREET

91ST STREET

92D STREET

93D STREET

HOUSING
PROJECT

99TH STREET

100TH STREET

101ST STREET

102D STREET

LOVE CANAL

SCHOOL

WHEATFIELD AVE.

RING II HOMES

RING I HOMES

RING I HOMES

RING II HOMES

103D STREET

FRONTIER AVE.

NIAGARA RIVER

BUFFALO AVENUE

AREA AFFECTED BY
FIRST EVACUATION

AREA AFFECTED BY
SECOND EVACUATION

1

THE PROBLEM AT LOVE CANAL

Almost everyone has heard about Love Canal, but not many people know what it is all about. The Love Canal story is about a thousand families who lived near the site of an abandoned toxic chemical waste dump. More important, it is a warning of what could happen in any American community. We have very little protection against the toxic chemical wastes that threaten to poison our water, our air, and our food. The federal and state governments have agreed to move away everyone who wants to move; but they didn't at first. We had to work to achieve that goal. Love Canal is the story of how government tends to solve a problem, and of how we, ordinary citizens of the United States, can take control of our own lives by insisting that we be heard.

I want to tell you our story—my story—because I believe that ordinary citizens—using the tools of dignity, self-respect, common sense, and perseverance—can influence solutions to important problems in our society. To a great extent, we won our fight. It wasn't easy, that's for sure. In solving any difficult problem, you have to be prepared to fight long and hard, sometimes at great personal cost; but it can be done. It *must* be done if we are to survive as a democratic society—indeed, if we are to survive at all.

In order to understand what happened at Love Canal, and to understand my part in it, you need to know more about the canal. The best way to introduce you to the canal and its story is, I think, to let you read the statement we wrote explaining ourselves to the thousands of people from all over the world who wrote expressing interest and offering their support and help. You will see that we financed our fight against the federal government and the state of New York with donations from individuals and with the proceeds from T-shirt and cookie-bake sales. You don't need money, but it helps; what you need most are determination, imagination, the conviction that you're right, and the knowledge that you are fighting not only for your family but also for the good of everyone.

The Love Canal story—its history, effects, impact on human lives, and our struggle for a remedy—is best summarized by the Love Canal Homeowners Association statement:

Love Canal Homeowners Association

WHO ARE WE?

We are residents and taxpayers of New York State, living in a small middle class community. We are a group of concerned citizens and environmentalists, worried about the effects of toxic wastes in our area, and across the country. Love Canal families have seen first hand what low level chemical exposure can do to our health and the environment, and want to help other people clean-up or avoid problems in their neighborhoods.

The Love Canal Homeowners Association, Inc., was formed in August 1978 and our membership consists of over 500 families. The Homeowners Association has been successful in getting action in their area, including the funds to allow all residents to evacuate the Love Canal area and move to a safe environment. Our new goal is to educate and assist other communities with their problems or others interested in the hazardous waste issue.

WHAT IS THE LOVE CANAL?

The Love Canal is a hazardous waste dump-site located in the center of a middle class community in Niagara Falls, New York. We are the first dump-site to be recognized, of the thousands of dumps across the nation. The Environmental Protection Agency has recently estimated there are about 30,000 to 50,000 toxic waste dumps across the United States.

THE HISTORY OF LOVE CANAL

In 1892 William T. Love (where the name Love Canal originated), proposed connecting the upper and lower Niagara River, by digging a canal 6 to 7 miles long, so he could harness the water of the upper Niagara River into a navigable channel which would create a man made water falls with a 280 foot drop into the lower Niagara River and therefore would provide cheap power. However, the country fell into an economic depression and financial backing for the project slipped away. Love then abandoned the project leaving behind a partially dug section of the canal. In 1920, the land was sold at public auction and became a municipal and chemical disposal site until 1953. The principal company that dumped their waste in the canal was Hooker Chemical Corporation, a subsidiary to Occidental Petroleum. The City of Niagara Falls and the United States Army used the site as well, with the city dumping garbage and the Army dumping possible chemical warfare material and parts of the Manhattan project.

In 1953 Hooker after filling the canal and covering it with dirt, sold the land to the Board of Education for $1.00. The deed contained a stipulation which said if anyone incurred physical harm or death because of their buried wastes, Hooker would not be responsible. Hooker continuously tells us they properly warned the city and the board, we wonder.

Soon after the land changed owners, home building began adjacent to the 16 acre rectangle which was once the canal. The families were unaware of Love Canal, when purchasing their homes. In 1955, an elementary

school was opened; it had been erected near the corner
of the canal.

Residents began to complain about children being
burnt, nauseous odors, and black sludge in the later
1950's, but nothing was done. It was not until the later
1970's that government finally decided to investigate
the complaints.

The State began to investigate the health and
environmental problems in the spring of 1978. Since
then we have had three major evacuations including two
emergency declarations from President Carter.

WHAT DOES THE CANAL CONTAIN AND HOW FAR HAS IT GONE?

There are over 200 different compounds that have
been identified so far, in and around the Canal. There
are at least 12 known carcinogens (cancer causing chemicals) some human, other animal. Benzene is one which
is well known for causing leukemia in people. Dioxin,
the most deadly of all chemicals, has also been found in
and around the Love Canal. Our Health Commissioner
characterized Dioxin as "The most toxic substance ever
synthesized by man." Dioxin is toxic in very minute
amounts and is found as a contaminant in Trichloro-
phenol of which there were over 200 tons buried in the
Canal.

Hooker admits to burying about 21,800 tons of
various chemicals in the Canal, but, this is all they will
admit to. The Army denies burying wastes, yet there
are residents who testified to seeing Army personnel
and trucks on site.

The extent of chemical migration is still in question. Many of the air, and soil and water tests have
found chemicals throughout a ten block residential area,
in our creeks and the Niagara River. We do not know if
all chemicals found were from Love Canal or another
dump, or even if further tests would find problems
eleven, twelve or thirteen blocks away.

WHAT ARE THE HEALTH EFFECTS?

After the first State Health Department studies were completed a health order was issued. On August 2, 1978, the Health Department recommended temporary relocation of *ALL* pregnant women and children under the age of two. This order was issued because of a high incident of miscarriages and birth defected children in the 239 families they studied. These families lived closest to the Canal. By August 9, 1978 Governor Carey permanently relocated these families purchasing their homes at replacement value.

On February 8, 1979, another evacuation order was issued for pregnant women and children under two in the outer neighborhood. Again, because of miscarriages, stillbirths, birth defects, and low birth weight babies.

On May 21, 1980, President Carter declared a health emergency because of an Environmental Protection Agency health study which showed an abnormal amount of chromosome breakage in the Love Canal people. (Chromosome breakage means an increased chance of getting cancer, or having a miscarriage, birth defected baby or genetic damage in your families.) This order allowed 810 families temporary relocation out of the neighborhood.

On October 1, 1980, President Carter signed a bill to evacuate *ALL* families permanently from Love Canal, not because of adverse pregnancies, chromosome damage or high chemical exposures, but because of mental anguish.

Our Association with the help of other scientists, conducted a health survey of our community. We were forced to do our own study because the governmental agencies would not conduct a good objective scientific study. We looked at the area as a whole, and found families who lived on underground streambeds had the highest incidence of disease, but also many families in the area were affected with an abnormally high rate of illnesses.

The results of our studies showed above normal amounts of miscarriages, 50–75% chance, while living in

Love Canal. A birth defect rate in the past five years to be 56%.

Also, an increase in Central Nervous System disease including epilepsy, nervous breakdowns, suicide attempts, and hyperactivity in children, a greater chance of contracting urinary disorders, including kidney and bladder problems, an increase of asthma and other respiratory problems.

Our most recent survey showed, out of the last 15 pregnancies in Love Canal women, we have had only two normal births. The rest resulted in a miscarriage, stillborn, or birth defected babies.

CONSTRUCTION

The remedial construction is designed to prevent water from soaking into the Canal, and halt the outward flow of chemicals into the community. The drainage system consists of eight inch perforated clay pipes, laid 12 to 15 feet deep, encircling the canal to intercept water. The contaminated water, then flows into a steel holding tank, treated on-site, by an activated charcoal system. The system was then covered with a clay cap about six feet deep. Top soil and grass was planted on the cap to finish the project. There are many problems with this system:

(1) At best it will contain wastes in the canal, it will not remove them.

(2) It will not remove or address any chemical wastes that have moved out into the ten block area or through the storm sewer system.

(3) There are no monitoring wells placed, therefore no one can tell us if it is even working.

(4) Will the clay crack, as it has done in the past, only to cause further contamination of our environment and threaten public health?

HAS GOVERNMENT LEARNED FROM LOVE CANAL?

_____No. The new federal regulations, RCRA*, allow

*RESOURCE CONSERVATION AND RECOVERY ACT.

new Love Canals to be built legally, maybe in your backyard. The only difference is the new landfills must be monitored, but not by a responsible agency. The owner of the dump, the guy who is making millions will be the watchdog, he is supposed to report any problems.

Government (EPA) refuses to use their authority to force industry to properly dispose of their wastes, and protect our health and environment. Why, because industry has power and money.

There are safe methods now which could be used to dispose of 80% of the wastes, through recycling, neutralizing or high temperature incineration. These processes have been proven to work in other countries in Europe. We can use the safe methods here if you, the taxpayer, voter, citizen, force the government to use their authority! *YOU*, have to help put a stop to industrial poisoning of America! Write your representative, join an environmental group in your area, or contact us. Together we can fight pollution, alone we will all suffer from it!

WHAT WILL NOW HAPPEN TO THE LOVE CANAL NEIGHBORHOOD?

The State and Local government would like to revitalize the neighborhood, after we leave. They are planning to resell our homes. Why, because no one will admit there is a health problem at Love Canal. They will only acknowledge a concern for pregnant women and children under two. The health studies have all been "whitewashed." We are trying to stop the revitalization program, but if we don't the nation will hear new cries for help from Love Canal in a few years.

When will they ever learn!

———————————

Our office is funded by donations from interested groups and individuals.

The Association has also printed a "Chronological,"

dating from April 1978 to January 1980. It sells for $5.00 plus $1.00 for mailing. We are in the process of updating the "Chronological" now and therefore the price will increase in the future.

The Love Canal Homeowners Association is also selling a T-Shirt as a fund raiser.

On the T-Shirt it states:

LOVE CANAL
Another Product From
Hooker Chemical

The T-Shirt sells for $5.00 plus $1.00 for mailing. It comes in Adult sized—Small, Medium, Large and X Large.

If you are interested in either of the fund raisers or in sending a donation please send to:

LOVE CANAL HOMEOWNERS ASSOCIATION
c/o Lois Gibbs, P. O. Box 7097
Arlington, Virginia 22207

Before Love Canal

If you drove down my street *before Love Canal* (that's what I call what happened to us), you might have thought it looked like a typical American small town that you would see in a TV movie— neat bungalows, many painted white, with neatly clipped hedges or freshly painted fences. The houses are generally small but comfortable; at that time ("before Love Canal" in 1978) they sold for about $30,000. If you came in the summertime, you would have seen men painting their houses or adding an extra room, women taking care of gardens, and children riding bicycles and tricycles on the sidewalks or playing in the backyards.

You would see something quite different today. Since Love Canal, the houses nearest the canal area have been boarded up and abandoned. Many have homemade signs and graffiti, vividly telling what happened to make this a ghost town. The once-neat gardens are overgrown, the lawns uncut. A high chain-link fence surrounds the houses nearest the canal. The area is deserted. The fence is a reminder of the 22,000 tons of poisons buried there, poisons that can cause cancer, that can cause mothers to miscarry or give birth to deformed children, poisons that can make children and adults sick, many of them in ways doctors only dimly understand.

When we moved into our house on 101st Street in 1972, I didn't even know Love Canal was there. It was a lovely neighborhood in a quiet residential area, with lots of trees and lots of children outside playing. It seemed just the place for our family. We have two children—Michael, who was born just before we moved in, and Melissa (Missy), born June 12, 1975. I was twenty-six. I liked the neighborhood because it was in the city but out of it. It was convenient. There was a school within walking distance. I liked the idea of my children being able to walk to the 99th Street School. The school's playground was part of a big, open field with houses all around. Our new neighbors told us that the developers who sold them their houses said the city was going to put a park on the field.

It is really something, if you stop and think of it, that underneath that field were poisons, and on top of it was a grade school and a playground. We later found out that the Niagara Falls School Board knew the filled-in canal was a toxic dump site. We also know that they knew it was dangerous because, when the Hooker Chemical Corporation sold it to them for one dollar, Hooker put a clause in the deed declaring that the corporation would not be responsible for any harm that came to anyone from *chemicals* buried there. That one-dollar school site turned out to be some bargain!

My Son Attending That School

Love Canal actually began for me in June 1978 with Mike Brown's articles in the Niagara Falls *Gazette*. At first, I didn't realize where the canal was. Niagara Falls has two sets of streets numbered the same. Brown's articles said Love Canal was between 99th and 97th streets, but I didn't think he meant the place where my children went to school or where I took them to play on the jungle gyms and swings. Although I read the articles, I didn't pay much attention to them. One article did stand out, though. In it, Mike Brown wrote about monkeys subjected to PCB's having miscarriages and deformed offspring.

One of his later articles pointed out that the school had been built over the canal. Still, I paid little attention. It didn't affect me, Lois Gibbs. I thought it was terrible; but I lived on the other side of Pine Avenue. Those poor people over there on the other side were the ones who had to worry. The problem didn't affect me, so I wasn't going to bother doing anything about it, and I certainly wasn't going to speak out about it. Then when I found out the 99th Street School was indeed on top of it, I was alarmed. My son attended that school. He was in kindergarten that year. I decided I needed to do some investigating.

I went to my brother-in-law, Wayne Hadley, a biologist and, at the time, a professor at the State University of New York at Buffalo. He had worked on environmental problems and knew a lot about chemicals. I asked him to translate some of that jibber-jabber in the articles into English. I showed Wayne, Mike Brown's articles listing the chemicals in the canal and asked what they were. I was really alarmed by his answer. Some of the chemicals, he said, can affect the nervous system. Just a little bit, even the amount that's in paint or gasoline, can kill brain cells. I still couldn't believe it; but if it *were* true, I wanted to get Michael out of that 99th Street School.

I went down to the offices of the *Gazette* and was surprised to learn how many articles there were on Love Canal. It not only surprised me, it panicked me! The articles listed the chemicals and described some reactions to them. One is damage to the central nervous system. (Michael had begun having seizures after he started school.) Another is leukemia and other blood diseases. (Michael's white blood cell count had gone down.) The doctor said that might have been caused by the medication he took for his epilepsy, but now I wasn't so sure. Michael had started school in September and had developed epilepsy in December; in February his white blood count dropped.

All of a sudden, everything seemed to fall into place. There's no history of epilepsy in either my family or my husband's. So why should Michael develop it? He had always been sensitive to medication. I could never give him an aspirin like a normal baby because he would get sick to his stomach or break out in a rash. I couldn't give him *anything* because of that sensitivity. If it were true that Michael was more sensitive than most other children, then whatever chemicals were buried under the school would affect him more than they did other children in the school, or even more than my daughter Missy, who has always been a strong, lively child. The chemicals probably would not affect Missy, at least not right away. I wasn't thinking then about long-term effects. (A year and a half later, Missy was hospitalized for a blood-platelet disorder, but later she was fine.)

I went over all the articles with Wayne, and decided Michael definitely should not attend that school—nor, for that matter, should any child. They shouldn't even play on that playground. Wayne was worried about his son Eric. He and my sister Kathy used to leave Eric for me to baby-sit while they were at work.

I was stunned that the school board had allowed a school to be built on such a location. Even today, it doesn't seem possible that, knowing there were dangerous chemicals buried there, someone could put up a *school* on the site. The 99th Street School had over 400 children that year, one of its lowest annual enrollments.

I was about to get my first lesson in dealing with officials. When I started, I was interested only in myself and my child. I didn't stop to think about the other children in the neighborhood. I considered sending Michael to a Catholic School, and I even looked into the possibility; but I'm not Catholic, and my husband Harry didn't approve of a strict religious education. Besides, there were plenty of other schools in Niagara Falls. We had a choice. My choice was to send Michael to another public school.

I called the superintendent of schools, and told him I wanted my son removed from that school. I explained what I believed was Michael's problem, his susceptibility to chemicals and drugs of all kinds. I also told him what I was sure he already knew, that the school was sitting on a toxic waste dump site. I repeated that I wanted Michael transferred. He could finish the school year; but he wasn't going to attend that school the next year.

The superintendent told me I couldn't do that. He couldn't transfer a child merely because the child's mother didn't want him to go to a particular school. I would need statements from two doctors, anyway. I thought that was ridiculous, that there was already reason enough for my child to be moved: the school was over a chemical dump site, and Michael had been sick *after* he started attending the school. But I went to my pediatrician and asked him for a statement. He agreed to send one to the superintendent. I also went to my family doctor and explained about the canal. I told her about my fears and about the change in Michael's health since he started attending the school. She also agreed to write a statement for the school.

After awhile, I called the superintendent back. He wasn't in;

he was at a meeting. It was the first of many calls. Finally, after I had called once or twice a day for two weeks, he returned my phone calls. It was a strange conversation. At first, he said he hadn't gotten the doctors' statements. Then he contradicted himself by referring to them. He said Michael could not be removed from the school, based on those statements, because the statements alleged that the area was contaminated. If the area were contaminated, then it wasn't only Michael who should be removed; all the children should be removed. The superintendent said that he did not believe the area was contaminated, and, finally, that they weren't about to close the 99th Street School.

I was furious. I wasn't going to send my child to a place that was poisoned. The thoughts that can go through a person's head. I thought that I, as a person, had rights, that I ought to have a choice, and that one of those choices was not to send my child to school in a contaminated place. Like many people, I can be stubborn when I get angry. I decided to go door-to-door and see if the other parents in the neighborhood felt the same way. That way, maybe something could be done. At the time, though, I didn't really think of it as "organizing."

It wasn't just the phone call with the superintendent that convinced me I had to do something. I called the president of the 99th Street School PTA and asked her if she could help me, or if she could at least tell me whom to go to or what to do. She said she was about to go on vacation. I got the feeling she wasn't interested. She seemed to be pushing me away, as if she didn't want to have anything to do with me.

I was disappointed and angry. School would open again in two months, and I wasn't going to let my child go back to that school. I didn't care what I had to do to prevent it. I wasn't going to send him to a private school, either. First of all, we couldn't afford it; and second, I thought parents had the right to send their children to schools that were safe.

Knocking on Doors

As I said, I decided to go door-to-door with a petition. It seemed like a good idea to start near the school, to talk to the mothers nearest it. I had already heard that a lot of the residents near the school had been upset about the chemicals for the past couple of years. I thought they might help me. I had never done anything like this, however, and I was frightened. I was afraid a lot of doors would be slammed in my face, that people would think I was some crazy fanatic. But I decided to do it anyway. I went to 99th and Wheatfield and knocked on my first door. There was no answer. I just stood there, not knowing what to do. It was an usually warm June day and I was perspiring. I thought: *What am I doing here? I must be crazy. People are going to think I am. Go home, you fool!* And that's just what I did.

It was one of those times when I had to sit down and face myself. I was afraid of making a fool of myself, I had scared myself, and I had gone home. When I got there, I sat at the kitchen table with my petition in my hand, thinking. *Wait. What if people do slam doors in your face? People may think you're crazy. But what's more important—what people think or your child's health? Either you're going to do something or you're going to have to admit you're a coward and not do it.* I decided to wait until the next day—partly to figure out exactly how I was going to do this but more, I think, to build my self-confidence.

The next day, I went out on my own street to talk to people I knew. It was a little easier to be brave with them. If I could convince people I knew—friends—maybe it would be less difficult to convince others. I started with the home of Michael's best friend, Curtis. His mother Kathy had gone over to her mother's with the children, but his father was at home. We talked and talked about the chemicals and the harm they could do. I think I talked more because of nerves and less because I had a lot to say. Finally, I asked him if he would sign my petition. I held my breath, waiting for him to say, "I won't, you're crazy!" But he signed. He agreed with me. He said: "I'm not going to send Curtis there, either. Curtis is hyperactive. If the canal does cause all the problems you say it does, because of the chemicals, well, maybe that's Curtis's problem. Maybe it isn't a psychological problem. Maybe it has something to do with the chemicals."* I was relieved—and pleased. I thought to myself, *Gee, this is going to be easy. I guess it isn't so bad after all.* I had a lot to learn.

At first, I went to my friends' houses. I went to the back door, as I always did when I visited a neighbor. Each house took about twenty or twenty-five minutes. They wanted to know

---

*In this book I am going to write as though people were actually saying certain things, because that's the way I remember what was said. I can't guarantee that they used exactly those words, but what they did say was similar to the way I have written it, and the meaning is the same.

about Love Canal. Many of the people who lived farther from the
canal than 97th or 99th streets didn't even know the canal existed;
they thought the area was a field. Some had heard about Love
Canal, but they didn't realize where it was, and they didn't pay
much attention to the issue—just as I hadn't. So I spent a lot of
time giving them the background, explaining what Love Canal was.
Something began to happen to me as I went around talking to
these people. It was hot and humid that summer. My mother
kept saying I was crazy to do it. I was losing weight, mainly because I didn't have much time to eat. My house was a mess because I wasn't home. Dinner was late, and Harry sometimes was
upset. Between the kids and the heat, I was getting very tired.
But something drove me on. I kept going door-to-door, still on
my own street. When I finished 101st, I did 102d; when I finished
those two streets, I felt ready to go back to 99th Street, where I
had begun by running home afraid of looking foolish.

Just before going back to 99th Street, I called a woman who
lived on 97th Street. Her backyard abutted the canal. I had
read about her in the newspaper. She was one of the people who
had been organizing others. She said she would be willing to help,
but nothing ever happened. Somehow something about her voice
didn't sound right. Although I didn't realize it at the time, I was
getting another lesson: even though we all have common problems, we don't always work together.

I shouldn't have been too surprised when I discovered later
that emergencies like this bring out the best and the worst in
people. Sometimes people have honest differences about the best
way to solve a problem. Sometimes, however, people have big
egos; it's more important for them to be up front and draw
attention to themselves than cooperate with others in working for
a cause. I really did have a lot to learn. At the time, there were
a lot of small groups organizing. Tom Heisner and Karen Schroeder, who lived right on the canal, had started getting people
together, and they were doing a good job, though we later had our
differences.

I started at the south end of 99th Street. It turned out that
that was the end of the canal most severely affected. The first
person I spoke to was Mr. Frain. I knocked on his door, introduced myself, and told him I had a petition demanding that the
school be closed down. Our children's lives were being threatened.
He understood right away and signed my petition. Then he
showed me the steps to his front porch. The steps had separated

from the house. They were about two inches lower than where they should have been and about an inch and a half away from the foundation. It looked as if the soil were sinking, but Mr. Frain didn't know why or what it meant. He asked me if I could talk to anyone, or if I could see if someone would come out and look at it. I didn't know what to do. Because he was so concerned, I told him I would try, and left.

It was terribly warm and humid that day. The closer I got to the canal, the more I could smell it. I could *feel* it, too, it was so humid. The odor seemed to hang in the thick air. My nose began to run, and my eyes were watering. I thought it was psychosomatic. I hadn't been eating properly and I was tired. Maybe, I thought, I'm just oversensitive. But my consciousness of the danger of the chemicals was not yet roused. Now I won't even drink the city water. I buy bottled water.

A Sick Community

As I proceeded down 99th Street, I developed a set speech. I would tell people what I wanted. But the speech wasn't all that necessary. It seemed as though every home on 99th Street had someone with an illness. One family had a young daughter with arthritis. They couldn't understand why she had it at her age. Another daughter had had a miscarriage. The father, still a fairly young man, had had a heart attack. I went to the next house, and there, people would tell me *their* troubles. People were reaching out; they were telling me their troubles in hopes I would do something. But I didn't know anything to do. I was also confused. I just wanted to stop children from going to that school. Now look at all those other health problems! Maybe they were related to the canal. But even if they were, what could I do?

As I continued going door-to-door, I heard more. The more I heard, the more frightened I became. This problem involved much more than the 99th Street School. The entire community seemed to be sick! Then I remembered my own neighbors. One who lived on the left of my husband and me was suffering from severe migraines and had been hospitalized three or four times that year. Her daughter had kidney problems and bleeding. A woman on the other side of us had gastrointestinal problems. A man in the next house down was dying of lung cancer and he didn't even work in industry. The man across the street had just

had lung surgery. I thought about Michael; maybe there *was* more
to it than just the school. I didn't understand how chemicals
could get all the way over to 101st Street from 99th; but the more
I thought about it, the more frightened I became—for my family
and for the whole neighborhood.

Everything was unbelievable. I worried that I was exaggerating, or that people were exaggerating their complaints. I talked it
over with Wayne. Luckily, he knew someone who might be able
to help us—a Dr. Beverly Paigen, who is a biologist, geneticist, and
cancer research scientist at the Roswell Park Memorial Institute, a
world-famous research hospital in Buffalo. We went to see Dr.
Paigen. She is a wonderful, brave person who, like Wayne, had been
involved in environmental-pollution fights. She asked us to bring
some soil samples so she could do an Ames test. The Ames test is
a quick way of determining potentially dangerous effects of
chemicals. When bacteria are exposed to mutagenic chemicals, Dr.
Paigen told us, they reproduce abnormally.

I continued to go door-to-door. I was becoming more worried
because of the many families with children who had birth defects.
Then I learned something even more frightening: there had been
five crib deaths within a few short blocks.

I was still getting people's cooperation and interest, but I was
soon to learn that not everyone felt the same way I did. The
woman on 97th Street who had done some organizing never
provided any help. We never argued; in fact, she never said
anything. One day, while I was knocking on doors, I noticed
her riding on her bicycle. She seemed to be watching me.
I was both puzzled and intimidated mainly because my self-
confidence wasn't yet all that high. I thought we had a
common problem, that we should be working together. But
she had tried to organize the neighborhood; therefore, it was
her neighborhood, her territory. Maybe she felt I was stepping on
her toes.

I finally got up my courage and walked over. "Hi," I said.
She was in front of her house. A tree in the front yard was wilted.
It looked sick, as though it were dying. We stood in the yard and
talked. She told me she couldn't use her backyard, that everything there was dead. She asked what I was doing, and I told her.
Her voice suddenly turned cold. She warned me about rocking the
boat, telling me not to make waves. She had already taken care of
the problem. She had been working hard, talking to a number of
politicians, and she didn't want me to undo what she had done.

I was taken aback. I explained that I didn't want to "undo" anything, that I wanted to work *with* her. It was a very hot day. I was dying of the heat. I wanted a cigarette or a cold drink—I didn't know which. There we were, standing in the hot sun, with the only shade coming from a dying tree, and she was telling me how everything was all right. I didn't know what to think. I had to go home and figure this out. I went home, but not because I was frightened. I just needed time to think, to figure out what was happening.

A Real Problem?

The New York State Health Department held a public meeting in June 1978. It was the first one I attended. Dr. Nicholas Vianna and some of his staff explained that they were going to do environmental and health studies. They wanted to take samples—of blood, air, and soil, as well as from sump pumps. They wanted to find out if there really was a problem. They would study only the first ring of houses, though, the ones with backyards abutting Love Canal. Bob Matthews, Niagara Falls city engineer, was there to explain the city's plan for remedial construction. They all sat in front of a big, green chalkboard on the stage in the auditorium of the 99th Street School.

I didn't understand everything that was said, especially about determining whether there was a problem. A pretty young woman carefully dressed, with a lovely scarf, spoke articulately. Her dog's nose had been burned when it sniffed the ground in her yard. She kept asking Dr. Vianna: "What does this mean? How did he burn his nose?" She said the dog was suffering, that her children loved the dog and loved playing with him; but she was willing to have the dog put away if Dr. Vianna would first test the dog.

That was a new reaction to me, one I hadn't come across in my canvassing. How *did* the dog burn his nose? Did that mean chemicals were on the surface? I knew there were health problems, and I felt the school should be closed; but I hadn't actually *seen* any chemicals. I felt a chill. This was a new danger, and a more ominous one. A man got up and said he couldn't put his daughter out in his own backyard because if he did, the soles of her feet would burn. The man thought chemicals were causing it.

His daughter was with him. She was a cute little thing, only eighteen months old, with curly dark hair. Imagine he couldn't let her play in his own backyard, and he didn't know why!

Dr. Vianna had no answer. "We are investigating. We will see what we can do." That was all he would, or could, say. When the audience realized that he didn't have any answers, the meeting became emotional. There were about seventy-five people in that warm, humid auditorium. Everyone was hot, and we could smell the canal. The heat must have had something to do with the short tempers. Next, Dr. Vianna advised people who lived near the canal not to eat any vegetables from their gardens. With that, the little girl's father became very upset. "Look—my kid can't play in the yard because her feet get burned. My neighbor's dog burns his nose in the yard. We can't eat out of the garden. What's going on here? What is this *all about?*"

Dr. Vianna just kept saying, "I don't know. We are investigating. It's too early to tell."

Then Bob Matthews discussed the remedial construction plan. He used the chalkboard to show us how a system of tile pipes would run the length of the canal on both sides. He said the canal was like a bathtub that was overflowing. He was talking to us as though we were children! He said it was like putting a fat woman in a bathtub causing the water to overflow onto the floor. The tile system would collect the overflow. Then it would be pumped out and treated by filtering it through charcoal. After it had been cleaned by the charcoal, it would be pumped down to the sewers and everything would be all right. The overflow-filtering system would also draw the chemicals away from the backyards, which would be clean again.

I asked him about the underground springs that feed into the canal. What would happen to them? He ignored the question, repeating, "It's like putting a fat lady in a bathtub." "That's not what I mean," I said, "I'm talking about *underground* streams. What happens to them? We are so close to the Niagara River. How will your overflow system shut those springs off?" Someone else observed that the tile drains would be only twelve feet deep. "What if the chemicals are forty feet down? The canal is probably forty feet deep." Another person said there were many types of chemicals in there. How was the city engineer going to get them out? No one would, or could, give us straight answers. The audience was getting frustrated and angry. They wanted answers.

I asked Dr. Vianna if the 99th Street School was safe. He answered that the air readings on the school had come back clean. But there we were, sitting in the school auditorium, smelling chemicals! I said: "You are telling me there are chemicals there. You are going to build this big, elaborate system to take the fat lady out of the bathtub and collect all this overflow. You tell us the air tests clean. But you also tell us we can't eat the vegetables. How can these kids be safe walking on the playground? How can it be safe?" "Have the children walk on the sidewalk," Dr. Vianna said. "Make sure they don't cut across the canal or walk on the canal itself."

I couldn't believe what I was hearing. I asked again: "How can you say all that when the playground is on the canal?" He didn't have an answer. He just said: "You are their mother. You can limit the time they play on the canal." I wondered if he had any children.

By now the audience was really frustrated, and so was I. People began walking out, muttering, furious. There were no answers. They didn't understand, and they were becoming frightened.

No Slamming Doors in My Face

Residents who hadn't attended the meeting heard what was going on by word of mouth. Everybody was very curious. A twenty-minute stay to get someone to sign my school petition turned into an hour or an hour and a half, and sometimes longer. People wanted to know what I knew, whom I had talked to, how things were going to be done. And they didn't know whom to turn to for answers. They had this or that illness; they had problems. Whom could they talk to? I was still trying to get my school petition finished. As the visits got longer, I began to feel I would never get through with the first ring of homes around the canal.

I clung to the idea of a school petition because I didn't know what else to do. Getting the names was a big, awesome job. I had never done anything like it before. But people kept asking me, and all I could do was listen. My heart went out to them. I said, "Yes, I will find out." But how was I going to find out? I didn't even know whom to ask.

Dr. Vianna was driving around the neighborhood in a big, white Department of Environmental Conservation (DEC) van with

"Environmental Studies" painted on the side. He was taking blood samples and doing a door-to-door health survey of people living in the first ring of houses around the canal. I asked him whom to contact for answers to my questions. He gave me his card and said that any time I had a question, he'd be willing to try to answer it. He seemed very nice, at that time.

It was a little easier to go back now that I had Dr. Vianna's card. The interviews were getting longer. In addition to their children and the school, people were worried about property values, about their homes. I still wanted to contact all the houses. Meanwhile, I was baby-sitting Wayne's and Kathy's son, Eric. So I took him and my two children on the visits. Interviews took less time with them along. People were less inclined to prolong a discussion when children were running around screaming, yelling, or running over their things with tricycles.

When I took Michael to 99th Street, his eyes swelled up. He looked puffy in general. His whole body seemed to have swelled up. His nose ran and he kept getting a bloody nose. I couldn't take him with me anymore. It made him sick. That convinced me of the truth of everything the residents were saying. They weren't exaggerating about children with birth defects. I left Michael at home, but I took Missy and Eric. I realize now that I shouldn't have done that. But at the time, I thought Michael was just particularly sensitive. I had to go on, however, so I left Michael with his grandma, or with his daddy, or with whoever was around. I took the other two with their little tricycles, and away we went.

By now I had contacted some 100 homes without a single door being slammed in my face. That had built up my confidence; it made me feel I was doing the right thing. Some people weren't deeply concerned, but they let me in, and many signed the petition. At least no one slammed the door in my face.

The first house on 97th Street had a large dog that barked a lot. The house was on a fenced-in lot and had an above-ground pool in the back. I wasn't about to try to get around that dog. I started toward the next house. Just then a van pulled into the driveway. The woman driving it was an old school friend. "Hi, Debbie," I said. "I remember you. You used to be Debbie Hoff." We talked awhile about old times. Then I told her what I was doing. Debbie Cerrillo invited me in for a cup of coffee. Her home was lovely. On the floors was thick orange carpeting. Everything was neat and well kept; some of Debbie's beautiful macrame was on the wall. We talked for a long time. Finally, I asked Debbie if she would be willing to take some petitions around. She thought there might be a problem, mainly because many people had moved there because the 99th Street School was within walking distance. But she would give it a try. She wasn't sure what she should say, so I wrote everything down. About all she would have to do would be read it. I had come a long way. Here I was encouraging Debbie to go out and do something that had terrified me. Soon she and I were close friends. She became vice-president of the Homeowners Association, remaining active even after the state bought her home.

I was meeting regularly with my brother-in-law Wayne and with Matt Murphy and John Daly, both members of the New York State legislature. On Friday mornings, we met at eight around my kitchen table and had coffee. Matt and John were most helpful. They gave us a lot of ideas about how to go about petitioning the state, seeing people, and in general getting action. They also made suggestions about whom to contact. At the same time, I kept them informed. Nineteen seventy-eight was an election year, and it was to their benefit to be informed. Beyond that, however, Matt Murphy and John Daly were genuinely concerned. Neither one was doing it just for votes. We sat around the kitchen table and talked strategy.

I had been in touch with Senator Patrick Moynihan's office. The senator's assistants assured me that they were doing everything they could, that the senator was preparing bills. Wayne suggested I follow up with a personal letter. Maybe then Senator Moynihan would answer. I asked him for help, for information about people to contact, about what he could do for the people in the Love Canal area. Senator Moynihan did write back. He said he was investigating the problem, that he would be in touch, and that he would keep us informed.

We also decided to talk to a lawyer and initiate a lawsuit. At first, we didn't know whom the lawsuit would be against. It turned out to be the City and the Board of Education of Niagara Falls, the County of Niagara Falls, and the Hooker Chemical Corporation. Wayne recommended Richard Lippes, an environmental lawyer who was an officer of the Sierra Club. I called and made an appointment for myself and two of my neighbors from 99th Street. One of the women had cancer, as did her daughter. The other neighbor had children with several health problems. The three of us drove to Lippes's office, which was in a beautiful old building with marble floors. The library in his office had high ceilings. There were hundreds of books and a huge conference table.

I had been in an attorney's office only once before, when we bought our house and then it was just in the outer office. I felt overwhelmed, but Rich was easy to talk to. We told him our problem. We asked what our chances were and if he was interested in taking the case. He said it would cost thousands of dollars to research a case like this, and, for that reason he didn't want to make any commitments. He wanted to read what we had, and would let us know. Fortunately, he took our case and became one of our most important advisors.

Now, when we went out on the street, we had more to say. Even if people didn't believe they had a health problem, or they didn't believe the canal was a problem, they *were* concerned about property values. And when people are concerned about their pocketbooks, they are *concerned.*

Rapidly Losing My Faith

Every time I went to another house, I learned something new. In one home, I met a graying, heavyset man with a pitted face. He couldn't walk very well. He had worked for Hooker at one time, and now he had chloracne, a condition that results from exposure to certain chemicals. I didn't know it then but chloracne is also a symptom of dioxin poisoning. Dioxin is toxic in parts per trillion. Later we learned that it was in Love Canal. The man was as nice and pleasant as he could be, but his face looked awful. It was all I could do to look at him. He wanted to go ahead with a class-action suit; but he was afraid to jeopardize his pension from Hooker.

I thought to myself: *How could you be so concerned about your pension? The law will protect you. Who cares about Hooker? Look what they've done to you in the plant, let alone what they've done to your family living here on one of their dump sites.* It was hard to understand why people were so afraid of Hooker, of what the company might do to them. Why weren't they angrier?

There were so many unbelievable things about the situation. In one house, a divorced woman with four children showed me a letter from the New York State Health Department. It was a thank-you letter, and a check was enclosed. I asked the woman what the check was for. She said the health department had contacted her and asked if her son would go onto Love Canal proper, find two "hot" rocks, and put them in the jars they sent her. She had been instructed to give the rocks to Dr. Vianna or to someone at the 99th Street School headquarters of the health department. The so-called hot rocks were phosphorous rocks that the children would pick up and throw against cement, and, in the process, burn themselves. The rocks would pop like fire-crackers. It amused the kids; but some had been burned on the eyes and skin. I just couldn't understand how a supposedly responsible agency would send an eleven-year-old child into a potentially dangerous area such as Love Canal and ask him pick up something there that could harm him. To get the rocks, he had to climb a snow fence put there to keep children out. It amazed me that the health department would do such a thing. They are supposed to protect people's health, and here they were jeopardizing an innocent child. I used to have a lot of faith in officials, especially doctors and experts. Now I was losing that faith—fast!

Our organizing effort was moving along. We had quite a few names, and I was getting help from Debbie. It was funny: I had gone out only a few weeks earlier with practically no self-confidence, not knowing what I was going to do or how I was going to go about it. And here was Debbie Cerrillo doing the same thing. It was like seeing myself all over again. She was shy about knocking on doors and cautious about what she would say. She was unsure of herself, but she did it, and she did a good job. She went to only three houses the first day; still, I thought that was great. It was more than I had done my first day.

People were gradually becoming aware of what was happening. They could hardly help it. The DEC van was going around, and people from the state were making a health survey and taking blood samples. I decided I would try to get my blood tested at the health department office set up at the 99th Street School. They had limited the testing to residents of 97th and 99th streets. Until now, I had been going to my own doctor for tests of possible liver or gall bladder problems. I wanted to have the test to find out what was wrong with me. Maybe my symptoms had something to do with Love Canal.

It was another hot day. The waiting line was long. A pregnant woman was standing in front of me. Why they didn't make appointments for people, I'll never understand. Anyway, I stood in line, filling out forms. I was afraid that if they found out I wasn't from 97th or 99th Street, they wouldn't give me the blood test. Just before my turn came, I collected the forms from the people around me and put mine in the middle, where my street would be less noticeable.

The pregnant woman lived on 99th Street. She was so afraid of the blood test that she practically pushed people ahead of her in line. I was annoyed; I had to get home so Harry could go to work. I began wishing the pregnant woman had pushed me in front of her. There were many children. They didn't want blood samples taken. Mothers had to force crying children to stay there. I've wondered since what will happen to all those children. Even if they are lucky and turn out to be healthy, will they have night-mares for the rest of their lives?

I wanted Harry to be tested also. I was worried that we were being affected even over there on 101st Street. Some of my neighbors thought it was silly to think we could be affected that far from the canal; but it was only a block and a half farther away. Most people on 101st said they wouldn't take the blood test. If I wanted to shut down the school, fine; but let's not carry it too far. "There's no problem over here," some said. "You have no business going over there. You're not a resident of 97th or 99th. Why don't you stay home and behave yourself!" Some of the women in the neighborhood would get together at a neighbor's house and gossip. "She's just doing it for publicity." But the gossip didn't bother me much. I was developing a pretty thick skin.

After weeks of carrying the petition door-to-door, one door *was* slammed in my face. It wasn't as bad as I had feared, though. The woman who answered my knock recognized me immediately. She really laid it on: "What are you out here for? Why are you doing this? Look what you're doing to property values. When did you put your house up for sale?" She was a bitter woman, but her attack wasn't on me personally. She was just letting me know how she felt. She wouldn't sign my petition. That was the worst encounter I had with a neighbor. By then, such a rebuff made almost no difference. I was disappointed that she wouldn't sign, but I didn't lose any sleep over it.

In July, the health department held another meeting. Dr. Vianna came, as did Dr. Steve Kim, a health department chemist, and some staff people. Bob Matthews was also there. They still had no answers. They merely urged people again not to eat vegetables from their gardens. As I went door-to-door, though, I found the people were still eating home-grown vegetables. "You shouldn't do that," I kept saying. "The health department says not to." The usual reply was that the health department was just trying to scare them.

The health department tried to explain its studies. The department had done liver tests and blood analyses, including white and red cell counts. They were relieved they didn't find what they had feared: leukemia or even very low, or fluctuating, white-blood cell counts. Leukemia is a form of cancer, and an abnormal white-blood-cell count is a symptom of leukemia.

But the health department still wouldn't say that the neighborhood was safe. Nor could they tell anyone what to do. Department officials were telling us: "Don't eat out of your gardens! Don't go in your backyard! Don't even go in your basement!" (In some houses, chemicals could be seen coming through the basement walls, and some people had had to replace sump pumps over and over because of corrosion.) It was at this point that the health department did something incredibly stupid.

Even today, I can't imagine what they had in mind. Maybe they thought they were being honest and open. They gave out air-sample results for individual homes. The results were in the form of a written list of chemicals—chloroform, benzene, toluene, trichlorethylene, tetrachlorethylene. Next to the names were some numbers. But the numbers had no meaning. People stood there looking at the numbers, knowing nothing of what they meant but suspecting the worst.

One woman, divorced and with three sick children, looked at the piece of paper with numbers and started crying hysterically: "No wonder my children are sick. Am I going to die? What's going to happen to my children?" No one could answer. The health department didn't even give her the OSHA standards provided by the Occupational Safety and Health Administration. I went over to calm her down. I told her that, based on what I had learned from Dr. Paigen and from Wayne, it might be a good idea for her to stay with a relative until the health department finished evaluating the area. She calmed down somewhat, but she was already very nervous and this uncertainty didn't help.

The night was very warm and humid, and the air was stagnant. On a night like that, the smell of Love Canal is hard to describe. It's all around you. It's as though it were about to envelop you and smother you. By now, we were outside, standing in the parking lot. The woman's panic caught on, starting a chain reaction. Soon, many people there were hysterical.

I talked to Dr. Kim. He was responsible for the environmental testing. I didn't know what chloroform did. I knew about benzene because Harry worked with it in his job, but I wasn't familiar with any of the other chemicals. "What do we do with these air readings? I don't know anything about them." Dr. Kim said they didn't mean anything. Some are very high, above OSHA standards. They were going to have an open meeting in Albany on August 2. He said we should be able to get interpretations of the data there. By then, they would have the epidemiological study practically finished, at least the miscarriage and birth defect data, and maybe some of the other tests.

I went back to collect air-sample readings. I hadn't met everyone before, and some wouldn't give them to me. One man went around saying, "Give it to Mrs. Gibbs. She's on our side." At that moment no one knew who was coming or going, or who was on what side. It was total confusion.

I managed to collect many of the readings. Wayne and some other people who understood them were shocked. They couldn't believe some of the readings, especially those for the woman who was so hysterical.

The meeting had one good effect: it brought people together. People who had been feuding because little Johnny hit little Billy were now talking to each other. They had air readings in common or a dead plant or a dead tree. They compared readings, saying, "Hey, this is what I've got. What have you got?" The word spread fast, and the community became close-knit. Everywhere you looked, there were people in little groups talking and wondering and worrying.

A Meeting in Albany

We decided to prepare for the August 2 meeting. By this time, Debbie Cerrillo was very active. So was Kathy Aul; but Kathy was pregnant, so she was limited in what she could do. We asked people in the neighborhood for questions we could take to the meeting.

When I first heard about the meeting, it didn't really register. It hit me when I got home. I thought: *This will be an open meeting. It will be for Love Canal residents. It is for people who*

live HERE. *It will be open to the public.* So why are they holding
it in Albany, 300 miles away? The answer, of course, was that
fewer people could attend the meeting.

I called Senator Moynihan's office. Could he use his influence to have the meeting moved to Niagara County so the people
who were involved, the people whose futures were at stake, could
go? Then I called Congressman John LaFalce's office. I called the
governor's office. I got nowhere. The meeting place remained un-
changed.

The woman who was organizing on 97th Street was still
riding up and down on her bike, wondering why I was working her
territory. She had everything under control, she said. "The
construction is going to work," she said. "Don't rock the boat,
Lois." When I told her I was going to the August 2 meeting in
Albany, she looked startled. Mr. Green, from Hooker, would fly
her there; she wasn't going to drive.

I was upset. *If she can go to Green, I can go to Green.* Then
I thought: *No. I don't want any part of Hooker. They're the
ones who've done the damage. I'm not going to ignore that. I'd
rather drive up on my own and be my own person.* I didn't know
what the other woman was thinking. Maybe she really believed
what the state was telling her, that everything would be all right.
She *didn't* want to rock the boat. She hadn't used her backyard
in seven years; but with the remedial construction, she thought
it would be possible to use it again. Somehow, because she liked
her home, there wasn't that much of a problem.

We continued our preparations for the meeting. I realized
that I had to know what I was talking about. I read all the articles
I could find on the canal and its problems and about everything
people had been talking about doing for the past couple of years.
I learned as much as I could from Wayne about the chemicals in
the homes and about their effects. I wrote out the questions I
wanted to ask. I didn't know then about the "swales" (covered
drainage ditches that once led away from the canal); what I
wanted were answers to questions about the underground springs.

Debbie Cerrillo, Harry, and I left for Albany on August 1. We
had a folder filled with news clippings Debbie and I had read.
We had questions from our neighbors. I was intimidated by the
meeting—me, Lois Gibbs, a houswife whose biggest decision up to
then had been what color wallpaper to use in my kitchen. Now,
here I was going to Albany. It didn't seem real. I was a little
nervous, so we stopped at Wayne's house for moral support. He

told us we would do a great job. If we wanted press coverage (we were beginning to understand that the press was our best friend), we should make our bid for it in the first fifteen minutes of the meeting or the early part of the open meeting—because that was about the only time the press would be there. Wayne told us to use our common sense. "Don't try to be an expert. You don't have to be a doctor or a toxicologist. Just use your head." The visit with him helped a lot.

Before leaving, we went by a drugstore and bought a whole bunch of junk food—candy, pop, and potato chips—which we stuck in the back of our 1972 Olds convertible. We had a good time all the way to Albany, laughing and singing and joking; but whenever we read the newspaper articles, we became sober.

Some of the articles were horrifying. If you have any heart at all, they grab you. I'd say to myself, "How could they do this? How could they let this continue?" Debbie Cerrillo had had two or three miscarriages and still occasionally suffered from heavy bleeding. There was an article about the monkeys' miscarriages and their offspring being born deformed, and Debbie Cerrillo was living right there. She had miscarriages, and the health department and some of the politicians knew what was in the canal. It was truly shocking. As early as 1976, a Calspan report had stated that dangerous chemicals were leaking out of Love Canal. Calspan, a private research laboratory hired to test in the area, had made numerous recommendations, but none had been followed.

I was learning that you can't trust government to look out for your interests. If you insist to government officials strongly enough, they *might* do the right thing. The Niagara County Health Department and other government officials had known about the pollution problem at Love Canal for a long time but had ignored it. Maybe it was the state's fiscal deficits or the blizzard of 1977. Whatever the reason, it was ignored, and the public's health was thereby jeopardized.

We stopped at every rest stop on the way to Albany. Harry is a professional at rest stops. He loves to go in, buy coffee, and sit and chat. What is normally a five- or six-hour ride took us about twelve hours. But we had a good time. When we got to Albany, we were flabbergasted. None of us had ever been there before. We didn't know where we were. We wanted to find the South Mall Campus, where the state government buildings are concentrated. When we had located it, we would find a hotel.

That way, it would be easy to get to the meeting the next morning.

We found the mall, drove through it, and went out the other side. The mall is beautiful at night. It's a white concrete mountain with lights. On the other side is a slum, with people hanging out windows or sitting on stoops drinking beer or wine. I felt uneasy and locked the car door.

There we were in the state capital with its large beautiful buildings that reminded us somewhat of a city in a science-fiction movie. They must have cost billions. On the other side, however, right next to the state capital, were poor people who spent their lives in crowded dingy buildings. Something is wrong with the way we do things, I thought.

We drove through the slum and into a strange park. I was driving, and Harry and Debbie were giving me directions; but we were going nowhere fast. We saw a taxi driver and asked him where a good hotel was. He sent us to another slum area. A policeman then directed us to a nice hotel, but it cost a fortune. It cost $40 a night, and we just didn't have that kind of money. At the time, Harry was taking home about $150 a week. Forty dollars, therefore, was a lot of money for us—that, plus gas, tolls, and other miscellaneous expenses. We went in anyway. We had no choice. Luckily, Debbie had a Master Charge card. As it turned out, we had only about $60 among the three of us.

It was about three in the morning by now, and the meeting started at nine. We had to leave by 7:30 A.M. in order to get breakfast and get there on time. Debbie, Harry, and I all shared one room because it was cheaper. I went over some of the questions and then climbed into bed. I knew I had to be prepared.

The Bombshell—Moving Out Pregnant Women

The following morning we drove to the mall. In the daylight, it seemed even more incredible. It's immense. Inside, it looks like a spaceship. The corridors made us feel as if we were in a huge cement-and-tile maze.

We went to Dr. David Axelrod's office, where we were told the meeting would be downstairs in a larger room because of the 161 Love Canal residents who were expected. We had brought a petition with 161 *names* on it; there was no need for the big conference room. The lady from 97th Street was already in the

room. She didn't seem happy to see us though. By conicidence,
she and I were wearing identical shirts!

Commissioner Robert Whalen, Dr. Vianna, Dr. Axelrod (who
would become the next health commissioner), Dr. Kim, and a few
others were sitting on the stage. Commissioner Whalen stood up
and began the meeting. He read an order stating that the residents
of Love Canal were not to eat food from their gardens and that
the 99th Street School would be closed during remedial construction. The bombshell came when he recommended the evacuation
of pregnant women and children under the age two because, he said,
the state was concerned about a danger to their health. Whalen
backed up this statement with data and statistics. He didn't say
the state *would* move all those people, just that they *should* move.
The state order stipulated only pregnant women and children
under the age of two. What, I wondered, were the rest of their
families supposed to do—leave them there?

With that I almost lost my cool. Then I remembered what
Wayne had said about the press and the first fifteen minutes.
Still, I was furious. I jumped up and said to Commissioner
Whalen: "If the dump will hurt pregnant women and children
under two, what for God's sake, is it going to do to the rest of us!?
What do you think you're doing?" Now very emotional, I said;
"You can't do that! That would be murder!" Debbie joined in:
"Wait a minute, wait a minute. My kids are *over* two. Are you
trying to tell me my children are safe?" (Debbie's backyard was
right on the canal. If the commissioner had made his decision
two months earlier, he would have moved her, but not now.)
Between the two of us, we kept the meeting in an uproar for
some fifteen minutes. "We can't eat out of our garden. We can't
go in our backyard. We can't have children under two. We can't
be pregnant. You're telling us it's safe for the rest of us!"

Commissioner Whalen left for a ten-minute break. He said
he would come back, but he didn't, and that made me angry all
over again. In the meantime, I talked to Dr. Vianna. He walked
up and down, up and down, insisting that he couldn't find any
problem. There just wasn't that much abnormality. I told him
I thought he was dead wrong. I had learned about five crib deaths
myself, just by walking around, and I wasn't doing a health survey.
Many women told me they had miscarried. I found sick people
all around the canal. "You can't stand there and tell me there's
no problem at Love Canal!" According to his survey, he didn't
see any. I kept telling him the survey must not have been con-

ducted properly. I told him about the five crib deaths, that most of those women had been breast-feeding. Dr. Vianna kept pacing. "You'll just have to get the residents to fill out health forms and sign them," he said. "You'll have to push the residents if you want to get anything done." In his own way, he was trying to be helpful; at the same time, he wasn't giving us any assurances.

When the meeting reconvened, Frank Rovers of Conestoga Rovers was on the stage to explain the remedial construction plan. He was the engineer who had drawn it up. I was still boiling from my talk with Dr. Vianna, and I now attacked Rovers. "Wait a minute," I said; "What about the underground streams?" He said they would be taken care of and gave me a technical explanation I didn't understand. "Excuse me," I replied. "I'm just a dumb housewife. I'm not an expert. *You're* the expert. I'm just going to use a little common sense. You will have underground streams running through the canal beneath those pipelines. The chemicals will get out. There's no way they are going to go into your pipe. They will be *under* it. Now, how do you *take care* of that?" He answered with some more incomprehensible engineering terms.

The meeting had been scheduled to last half an hour, but we made it last until well after the lunch hour. By then, Debbie and I were furious. Commissioner Whalen had walked out of the meeting, and these guys were giving us a bunch of baloney. I had a list of fifty questions, but all I got was engineering jargon and political answers that made no sense. "Well, we're going to check on that...." "According to the data available...." "We are going to evaluate that at a later date.... " "We're doing more studies.... " "We haven't got everything completed yet.... " "You're going to have to be patient.... " Yet the newspaper reports said they had been doing studies since 1976, or even before then, and here it was two years later, and they were telling us they needed to study the problem some more.

Toward the end of the meeting, Dr. Axelrod told me he would hold a public meeting the following day in Niagara Falls to explain the situation to the residents. He asked me if I would have any people there. I told him I would pack the auditorium. "I don't think you can get that many people out," he replied. I said: "I'll make sure there is standing room only." I didn't know whether he was challenging me or giving me a message, that the government would respond only to a large number of angry people. As it turned out, Commissioner Whalen's order guar-

anteed a full house. I don't know what else they thought would
happen when they said pregnant women and children under age
two would be moved. Did they think no one would notice it?

We started home. We were so angry that none of us—Debbie,
Harry, or I—could speak coherently. What we did instead was
listen to the tape we had made of the meeting. The more we
listened, the angrier we got. We drove straight through, making
only one rest stop. We stopped mainly so Debbie could call her
mother and her husband and tell them she was on the way home—
that everything was fine, we hadn't had any car accidents or anything like that. After the call, Debbie and I went to the ladies'
room. Debbie was in one stall and I was in the next. Debbie said
her mother had told her she thought the 97th Street woman was
in collusion with Hooker. Debbie asked what "collusion" meant.
I said it meant that the woman was *bought and paid for* by the
Hooker Corporation. (I know now that was not true.) Debbie
started cursing. "That SOB! How can she do that? Doesn't she
care about other people?" "Yeah," I said sarcastically, and we
talked back and forth. I stepped out of the stall to find the
97th Street woman standing there. She too was driving back,
in spite of all that talk about flying. To warn Debbie, I said very
loudly: "Well, hello, 97th Street" Debbie, who is a large woman,
made herself as small as she could. She waited until she could
hear the woman go into another stall, and then Debbie snuck
out. It was embarrassing but also funny.

I learned something from that incident. I vowed right then
and there that I wouldn't say anything in public that I didn't
want heard.

A Street Meeting

When we got back to Niagara Falls, we drove to my house to see
the kids. My mother was standing on the sidewalk, waving both
arms. "Get right over to 99th Street," she yelled. "They're
having a street meeting. They've all gone crazy." I thought my
mother had gone crazy, standing there in the middle of the street
yelling at me. I was exhausted. We had had two or three hours
sleep, and we had been driving much of the day. It had been an
emotional meeting. I had just about had it. I had to push myself
to do anything. I had to push myself every inch of the way. I
didn't want to go, but she was so excited. So I said: "OK, fine."

Wayne and Kathy had told people we were on our way back from Albany. We drove up Colvin, then down 99th. We went down 97th Street, but I still didn't see anything. Then, at Wheatfield, the road was blocked. Hundreds of people were in the street, screaming, yelling, and talking—and burning papers in a bucket. I had never seen anything like it. They were like a mob, feelings were running so high. When I saw Wayne and Kathy, I got out of the car.

Tom Heisner was standing on a box, holding a microphone. "Is Lois Gibbs back from Albany yet? Is Lois Gibbs back from Albany?" I walked around hoping no one would notice me. Wayne and Kathy said they had heard about the health commissioner's statement on the radio. "It's wild. There's no one here from the health department, or any department, to explain what it means." Just then somebody in the crowd recognized me and pushed me up to the microphone.

I had never spoken to a group of people in my whole life. In high school, if I had to do a book report in front of the class, I would cut the class. It just wasn't my way. Nevertheless, I introduced myself to Tom and Lois Heisner. Tom Heisner was telling people to burn their mortgages, to tear up their tax bills. "We're not paying anything. This house is worthless, useless. It's not worth anything. It's no good. It's uninhabitable. We can't live here." And a lot of residents were doing it. They were bringing up papers and putting them in a bucket to be burned.

I was nervous. I had a habit of saying "OK" after everything I said. I would say "OK? I'd like to talk to you, OK? I'd like to talk to you about something that is going on, OK?" It was a speech habit, or maybe I had so little confidence in myself that I was asking people for permission to speak. Wayne took it upon himself to cure my habit by sticking his finger up every time I said OK—to make me conscious of what I was saying. Wayne sensed I could become a leader; in his own way, he was trying to train me.

I got up to the microphone and stood there looking out at about 400 people. Some were pregnant women, some little children, some senior citizens; there were people of all ages, colors, sexes, and sizes. Tom Heisner introduced me. All those faces were looking up, waiting for me to say something. You could hear a pin drop. Everything was quiet. Looking at all those people, all I could think of was *What am I going to tell you?* I'd never been so furious at a meeting in my life. *How can I tell you that something good is going to happen, that it's going to be OK for you, that we are going to work together to get us all out of here?* I stood there a minute. All eyes were on me.

I grabbed the microphone. It started to squeal. Someone told me to take my hands off it; that's what was making the microphone squeal. I looked out at the people and said, "OK." Wayne stuck his arm up in the air, with one finger showing. I thought to myself: *Oh boy, I'm off to a good start. That's all I need, for Wayne to stand there with his fingers up.* I grabbed the microphone again because of Wayne's finger and it squealed and squeaked. Everyone was getting a little restless. I told them that as they already knew, Commissioner Whalen had issued an order for pregnant women and children under two to be moved from the area temporarily. He issued the order because they had found an above-normal number of miscarriages and birth defects in the area. Pregnant women and children under two were particularly vulnerable. He also recommended that the 99th Street School be closed during construction.

Everytime I said, "OK," Wayne stuck a finger up. I think he got up to six fingers during my speech. I don't know if he missed any, or just ran out of fingers and started all over again. It could have been sixteen, for all I knew.

I went on. The reason they said they couldn't evacuate more people was that the data were insufficient, according to Dr. Vianna. I told them I knew five crib deaths but that Dr. Vianna had recorded only two. If there were things they hadn't put on their health surveys, call Albany or notify one of the doctors. "Tell them everything. If you had three pimples this time last month, and this time you have five—tell them!" I said that because many people were embarrassed to tell doctors such personal things. "If you have a problem, or if you have colds above normal, or headaches—anything—call Albany and tell them." A lot of people didn't connect all this with chemicals. Dr. Paigen had told me, however, that chemicals can reduce a person's resistance. "If your children have eye problems, or feet problems, or birth defects, let them know. Put it in writing. They need to know. We need to cooperate with the health department." At the time I still believed it was an honest game, that the straightforward approach was best, that the reason everyone was not being moved was that the health authorities did not have all the information, that once they did, everyone would be moved.

Some residents didn't want to hear that. They just wanted to get out. A pregnant woman was standing there crying. "What's going to happen to me, Mrs. Gibbs? What's going to happen to my baby? I am already five months pregnant. Look at my stomach. This baby's already been through the first three months. What's going to happen to my baby? Should I get some more tests? Is it going to be all right? Is it going to have a birth defect?" Other women, those with children under two (or over two), wondered what had already happened to their children, to their bodies or their brains. Would they die of leukemia? Would they get some other form of cancer? Would they have a crippling disease? If they had children, would their children be able to have children?

Those were the questions people asked. The health department had no one there, and I certainly couldn't answer such questions. I tried to sympathize with them and explain what I had learned (practically nothing). That seemed to ease their minds a little bit. Meanwhile, Wayne was sticking up his fingers, and the microphone was squealing. I told everyone that some state officials were coming to hold another meeting tomorrow, that they should go to 99th Street School auditorium, where the state experts could answer their questions.

In hindsight, it's almost impossible to describe that evening. It was horrible to see all those people so afraid, helpless, and angry, not knowing what to do or where to turn. When I finally sat down at home, it was the first rest I had had in a long time. I talked things over with Wayne and played the tape of the Albany meeting for him. He thought it was great, that I had timed the outburst perfectly for the press. He assured me that everything would be fine. I respected Wayne's opinion, and I needed the reassurance. I fell asleep as soon as Wayne and Kathy left.

Governor Carey Absent?

The following morning we sent out a flier to let everyone know there would be a meeting at the 99th Street School. Mr. Copy donated the service. The flier told everyone to attend. I was hoping for 500 people. There were about a hundred homes right around the canal. I was afraid people from the nearby streets wouldn't turn out. But they did!

That day, my house was like Grand Central Station with

papers all over the place; and there were air readings, phone calls, and people coming and going. I didn't realize it then, but that scene would be repeated over and over. I don't think we had a clean coffee cup for months and months. The house was dirty. This really bothered me. Before Love Canal, my house was immaculate. There wasn't anything out of place. Before Love Canal, not many people came to our house, other than family and a few friends. Now I had residents, neighbors, politicians, and various important people. And I couldn't keep the floor clean. All those VIPs and my house looked like hell!

We went to the meeting early the next evening and stood near the door of the school in the shade of the building. It was the only cool place; there wasn't a shade tree around. It was warm and humid—85 degrees outside, and the humidity was over 90. We talked outside with some of the residents and then went in to the meeting. It was just as hot inside and the auditorium was packed—standing room only. Even before the meeting was called to order, the audience had become emotional. Some were worried and some were crying; some, probably from nerves, cracked jokes.

The officials all sat on the stage. Tom Frey conducted the meeting on behalf of the governor's office. Commissioner Whalen got about a quarter of the way through reading his order when people started firing at him. "Look, we already heard your order. We want to know what it means!" One man stood up, grabbed his wife's arm, stood her up and started yelling: "What does that mean for my wife who is eight months pregnant? What does that mean for her? It's too late for her!" This man actually had tears in his eyes. I think it was to be his first baby. His wife and his unborn baby were in danger and he had no control over it. "What are you going to do for her? It's too late!"

Lois Heisner was crying. "My daughter already has birth defects. She already has horrible illnesses. She is already sick. What are you going to do for her? She's already over three. Does that mean she has to stay and die? We have chemicals in our base-ment. You took an air reading. I've got this air reading and I don't even know what it means. Does it mean our lives are in jeopardy?" She just cried and cried. She looked so distraught, so helpless, pleading for help, and Tom Frey said, "Let's call this thing to order. One person at a time. We can't have everybody screaming and hollering." The more he said that, the angrier the crowd got. Everyone started screaming. The lady on the left was talking about her three-year-old, another about her unborn child, and another saying she wants to have children and is afraid.

Mrs. Taylor was still waiting for someone to do something about her dog. Albany kept promising they would take the dog to study it or to put it away. The dog was suffering and she wanted him put out of his misery, but she wanted something to be done with the animal so that it might help them with their studies. To this day, I don't know if any of the people from the state ever talked to her or explained anything.

About that time, I stood up and asked where Governor Carey was. "If it is an emergency situation, and you are telling pregnant women and children to leave, the governor should be here." Tom Frey said the governor was up for reelection and was campaigning. That almost blew the roof off. "What's more important, his campaign or the people in this room, these people whose homes are at stake, whose lives are at stake? What's more important to Governor Carey?" I demanded the governor come down; Tom Frey said he would ask him.

Everyone was emotional, myself included. Everywhere you looked someone was crying, or hysterical, or near panic. "I've got this air reading. What does it mean? I have a total reading of 1500 of these seven chemicals in my home. What does it mean? Does it mean I should leave today, leave tomorrow?" No one had any answers. "We don't know what it means. We don't have any standards for residential areas. We don't have any standards other than OSHA standards, and OSHA standards are made for men and for a forty-hour week. We don't have anything for a residential area." One woman expressed everyone's feelings when she said, "Then why did you give me this? If you don't know what it means, then don't give it to me."

The meeting that night lasted until well after eleven. Commissioner Whalen said only about two words through the whole thing. He kept looking down at me with an icy stare. I can't explain the feeling. I just stared back at him and thought: *Where do you get off judging everybody's future, telling people what they can and cannot do. You're not God.* It was the way they sat up there, so arrogant and so righteous. This is the way it's going to be. Too bad about your two-and-half-year-old. Too bad about your three-year-old.

Tom Frey said they were only going to move people temporarily. It was ridiculous. "You're going to move pregnant women and children under two. What are you going to do about the rest of the family? If it's dangerous for my wife and baby, you're going to leave me here with the other three children?" Finally, near the end of the meeting they decided to move the whole family. They realized they couldn't separate families.

After the meeting, a group went to my house. The press called me for a statement. "What is going on?" "What are your feelings?" "How did you make out in Albany?" Every TV camera and every newspaper from coast to coast was up here that day or the day after. *The New York Times* carried the story just before they went out on strike. Buffalo's four TV stations all came out. My phone never stopped ringing. Wayne took some of the calls so I wouldn't have to talk to everyone. He helped me prepare press statements to give to reporters including Paul MacClennan and Dave Shribman, both of whom wrote numerous important stories.

In one way, the whole thing was like a long, strange dream. I couldn't believe it. Me. What am I doing here? All I had wanted to do was move my child out of the school. I'm not the kind of person that does things like this. Why am I here? Why am I doing this? I was doing everything, but it was like someone else acting and I was watching.

The phones kept ringing and people kept arriving. I went to bed about 3:30 in the morning. That's when everyone left. The press started calling me at six. I had never dealt with them before and didn't know then about their deadlines.

It was all a new experience. It was exciting but also frightening. I wasn't sure what to do next or how to do it. Wayne was thinking of leaving the area and moving to Oklahoma or Montana. What would I do without him? I needed him to guide me, to put things in perspective, to tell me where to go and how to do it– to help me write press statements and think through strategies.

The Love Canal Homeowners Association

As you might imagine, people were pretty upset. They were talking and stirring each other up. I was afraid there would be violence. We had a meeting at my house to try to put everything together. We invited our attorney, Rich Lippes, and together we decided to form a homeowners' association. We got out the word as best we could and told everyone to come to the Frontier Fire Hall on 102d Street, within the Love Canal area, on August 4.

The firehouse was packed with people, and more were outside. It had been a very hot, humid day. It still hadn't cooled off. Several politicians came, including Mary Ann Krupsak, the lieutenant governor, who was running for governor in the primary. Some local people came. The health department had people there. I sat on the stage with Tom Heisner and Karen Schroeder. It was really chaotic for awhile. Everyone wanted to have his say. Wayne called the meeting to order. He began by saying we would like to start a Love Canal homeowners' association and that the boundaries would be from 93d and 103d streets and Buffalo Avenue to Bergholtz Creek. These were natural boundaries that made sense to everyone.

Wayne asked for nominations for officers from the floor. In the meantime, we passed out a yellow sheet of paper for people who wanted to join the association. We'd get their signature, and a dollar as a token membership fee. Rich Lippes was at the table in front with the others, and my sister Kathy was at the chalkboard writing down the names of people who were nominated for president. We took the vote. I was elected president and Tom Heisner vice-president. Karen Schroeder was elected secretary and Debbie Cerrillo, treasurer.

I took over the meeting but I was scared to death. It was only the second time in my life I had been in front of a microphone or a crowd. Just as I got to the microphone and started to say, "Good evening. I'm Lois Gibbs," Congressman LaFalce came crashing in and grabbed the microphone from me, or at least, that's the way it felt to me. He probably was a lot more polite than that. From somewhere I got up the nerve to tell him that we decided that politicians would speak at the end. He said he had an important announcement. Could he please have the microphone? I said all right and gave it to him.

He was trying to get four million dollars from the federal government. I was only half listening. It all seemed so crazy. Everyone was trying to get to the microphone. It was total confusion. All I could think of was "How am I going to get through this evening?" I wanted to get the goals set and to get some concrete things started, and it seemed like everyone wanted the microphone. Congressman LaFalce finished up with the TV cameras filming him.

We set four goals right at the beginning—(1) get all the residents within the Love Canal area who wanted to be evacuated, evacuated and relocated, especially during the construction and repair of the canal; (2) do something about propping up property values; (3) get the canal fixed properly; and (4) have air sampling and soil and water testing done throughout the whole area, so we could tell how far the contamination had spread. We discussed the goals and finally we voted and passed them. I wanted to use the time to answer questions, but first I introduced Richard Lippes. I suggested Rich as our association attorney. Rich introduced himself, gave his credentials, and was voted in as the association's lawyer.

Dr. Paigen spoke that night. I didn't know her too well then, but I liked her right from the start. She is a soft-spoken person, someone you feel you can trust. She was easy-going but not weak, as I was to find out later, when the crunch came. She offered advice about taking vitamins to counteract some of the effects of the chemicals, especially the carcinogenic ones. Considering all the confusion, though, I doubt many heard her.

Then all the rest of the politicians and others who represented organizations went to the microphone to say their pieces. Some were pretty nice, offering things like a place for us to have an office. One man talked about fund raising. Another volunteered something else. We got a list of about 550 names of people who wanted to join the association. I don't know how I got through that night. We didn't start home until eleven.

As we were walking home, Wayne or Beverly remarked that you could close your eyes and walk down the street and tell where every single storm sewer opening was just from the smell. It was true; even though I was in the midst of it, I still couldn't believe the contamination had reached my house.

There were a lot of things to do when we got home. I had to put all the papers away somewhere, and we had to send a telegram to President Carter on behalf of the association. Wayne helped me compose it. Actually, he pretty much wrote it. By this time, I was physically and emotionally exhausted. I didn't know if I was coming or going. My head was spinning. I had so many things on my mind. I had a list of things that should have been done. It was the first time in my life I didn't know what I was doing, or how I was going to do it.

It seemed like weeks or months since I had seen my kids. My husband was getting upset with me. I was never home. I was always somewhere else. Dinner was never on time. Harry didn't say anything, but I could tell he was annoyed. He would walk up and down with his hands in his pockets. He even began to get a little bit jealous because I was spending so much time away. I still couldn't believe it was all happening. Three months earlier, I didn't even know there was a problem. I never dreamed I would be in the middle of something like this. If anyone had told me that, I would have said they were out of their mind, that I just wasn't that type of person.

The VIPs

Well, it was real, it was happening every day, and it was happening quickly. The following morning, August 5, I received a call from the state department of transportation. Bill Wilcox, from the Federal Disaster Assistance Administration, and some other officials were coming in to evaluate the area and to talk with some of the residents. I didn't realize then that there were high-level "tourists," similar to the tourists who come to Niagara Falls and drive around the neighborhood to rubberneck out of curiosity. I didn't have much time to get dressed, but I did the best I could. I like to look nice, and I felt it was especially important to look nice when VIPs came around. I went over to Love Canal and waited for Wilcox to arrive. He was an older man, very open. He talked to you as if you were an adult, not as if you were a not-too-bright child, as some did.

We took him on a tour of the canal. I was on his one side and Debbie Cerrillo on the other. Wayne told us not to stop talking. "When Lois stops talking, Debbie, you take over, and vice versa." Well, Wayne usually knew what he was talking about, so that's what we did. I told Wilcox about Love Canal and the school being built there on the dump site, the problems with my boy, and the health problems in the neighborhood. When I stopped to catch my breath, Debbie started. It seemed funny at the time, almost like a game. These are the rules. There are your moves. If you don't stop talking, you'll win the game. I went along with it. I talked and Debbie talked.

We took him over to the Voorhees house. Joe McDougall, an engineer with the Niagara Falls City Water Department, was also on the tour. The Voorhees' basement had a raunchy smell that took your breath away. It was a distinctively Love Canal odor. We were standing by the sump pump; Joe McDougall was saying that if he were to stir up the sump pump, everyone in the room would get deathly sick. When he said that, I said, "Stir, Joe, stir! We want to show this stuff can create a disaster. Don't just stand there with that stick, stir it. For God's sake, stir it! We want to make them sick to show it is a disaster." But Joe just wouldn't stir it. I don't know if he thought I was kidding, but I was serious. Actually, Joe McDougall was one of the few people in government who tried to help, before the city gagged him.

We went over to the Schroeders' through the backyard. Bill Wilcox could see the gunk there. Then we cut across the canal to get to Debbie's house. Debbie and I made him a little paranoid, I think, because we told him to watch where he stepped. "Barrels are erupting. There are holes all over the place. Be careful you don't step in any goop." We showed him some of the holes. He got a sinus headache from the walk across the canal. He said he felt it immediately. As we went across the canal, we found one of those black holes that is so deep that you can't get a stick to the bottom of it. You pull the stick out and see black gunk its entire length.

We showed him the barrel that was coming to the surface right near Debbie Cerrillo's swimming pool and the hole with black gunk in her yard. Pete Bulka lived next door to Debbie. Pete had been complaining to the City of Niagara Falls for a long time, but nothing was ever done. Pete explained how his sump pump had to be replaced every few months because it corroded. The county health commissioner wanted to cap everyone's sump pump because they were pumping chemicals from the canal into the storm sewers and then into the Niagara River. He acted as if it were the citizens' fault that they were pumping poison into the river, that it was better that it just stayed in people's basements.

While we were down in Pete Bulka's basement, Congressman LaFalce was with us, and of course the press followed us around. They wanted to take photographs. They wanted us to hang our heads over the sump pump. The strong smell made my eyes water, my head hurt, and my ears ring. And they kept telling me to put my head down there one more time. If I did it one more time, I would have gotten sick to my stomach.

Mayor Michael O'Laughlin of Niagara Falls was on the school grounds, but he said nothing. Later on, he blamed us for hurting tourism in Niagara Falls. When we wanted help with our taxes, he said others wouldn't like it if we got a tax break and they had to pay more taxes.

We took Mr. Wilcox out on the playground to show him where the children had been playing, especially the ball field on top of the canal. Whenever residents complained that barrels were erupting on the playing field, or chemicals were surfacing, all the city did was fill in the hole with dirt.

After he left, I felt pretty good. We went home and talked for a little while; but the quiet didn't last. Residents were calling; the press wanted a comment. I feel embarrassed about some of the statements I gave then. I have a limited education, and my vocabulary isn't that large. I didn't know quite what to write or say. When anybody asked me for a comment, I felt inadequate.

Wayne helped me with the written statements. He pointed out the facts that are the most important and the things that should be said. I shouldn't have compared myself to Wayne; but I couldn't do what Wayne could do, and I felt dumb. He was trying to help me, but Wayne would make lists of things I did wrong, and I felt he was just nit-picking. I had enough pressure with people calling me and banging on my door. I was frustrated and was ready to chuck the whole thing.

Meeting the Governor

On August 7 Governor Carey came to Love Canal to meet with us. It was the first time I met him. We were all excited, waiting in the parking lot at the 99th Street School. People were still angry, and many were scared. Everybody was hoping the governor would bring us good news. Some said he was coming only because he was running for reelection. I was thrilled that the governor was coming and that I would have a chance to meet him. I had never imagined meeting or talking to or being anywhere near the governor of New York State.

His plane was two hours late getting into Niagara Falls Airport. It was hot, and by then, the people waiting were tired and irritated. I was annoyed. There were a lot of other things I could do than stand around a parking lot in the hot sun. My house was a mess. My kids needed attention. My laundry needed to be done, and I had calls to return. The governor was wasting my time.

When the governor finally arrived, Tom Frey introduced us and shook hands. We had a private meeting at the 99th Street School before the general meeting. Wayne, Karen Schroeder, Tom Heisner, the governor and some of his aides, and I sat around a table. I was flattered to be included in a private meeting. Tom started out by saying he wanted to be relocated, that the canal was a threat to his family. The governor then turned to me. Tom interrupted me twice. Finally, the governor, who was irritated, told him, in effect, to shut up. He looked at Tom as though he were going to throw him out of the room.

Then Governor Carey turned back to me. He has piercing eyes that stare right through you. I thought of the laser beams on *Star Trek*. He didn't smile at all, and he looked intimidating. I was thinking *God, what am I doing talking to this guy? He's a powerful man. He's sitting here next to me. From the look in his eyes, I can just tell he hates my guts*. I can't say he hated me, but he didn't plan to come here, and I was the one who embarrassed him by saying what I did. Whatever it was, I was nervous. It took all I had to say a few words about people needing to be relocated, that pregnant women and children—all of us—were being harmed. Wayne jumped in. In an organized, professional way, he said what needed to be said. I had mumbled and stumbled—or at least that's the way it felt to me.

I couldn't get over that piercing look, that stony face with no smile. It made me feel worthless. I don't know if that was what the governor wanted. I don't think so, but it is funny how ordinary people don't think that much of themselves. They put themselves down so much in front of important people. Well, I would learn that a lot of important people don't deserve the respect they get. Some are not honest and some do not care.

When the governor went into the public meeting, I never saw so much TV coverage. I was thrilled at the idea of being on TV. It was exciting. Later I would turn on the set, and there was my face on TV. During the session I sat in the front row of the auditorium. Governor Carey was up on the stage. Tom Frey then invited me to sit on the stage next to the governor. Commissioner Whalen, Transportation Commissioner Hennessy (who was going to head up the governor's task force), Tom Frey (the governor's assistant), and I were all on stage.

Tom Frey started the meeting. He was trying to recognize people one at a time, but people were shouting. The governor finally got up to the microphone. The residents were screaming and shouting. "You're a murderer! You're killing our children! You can't allow this to happen!" The governor was campaigning, and it didn't look good.

All of a sudden I heard Governor Carey say he would purchase the first and second ring of homes and that he would relocate the people. I don't know why he did it, whether it was the political campaign, or what, but he was very generous. He even told the residents that if their basements were contaminated, and they had furniture in the basements, he would pay for that as well. When he said it, I was really excited that people were going to get out. It was great.

I was startled by Tom Frey, who almost fell out of his chair. "Oh my God," he said, "I don't believe the governor said that!" I couldn't understand why Tom Frey said that. I knew that it had something to do with cost, but this was the governor talking. I thought: *Why should Frey be in shock? This is what is supposed to be. This is what being governor is about.* I was changing my mind. Despite those piercing eyes and icy stares, I was beginning to believe he was a good person. Later, I found out why Tom Frey was so shocked. It had to do with the fighting between the state and the federal agencies about who would pay. The governor had promised more than he had federal money to pay for.

Many of the other residents also wanted to be moved. Art Tracy, who lived on 102d Street, told the governor he wanted to be moved. The governor told him that if contamination and health problems were proven in areas away from the canal, the state would purchase those homes also. The residents on rings one and two were happy because their homes were going to be bought. The people past 99th and 97th streets were relieved to know that if the studies showed contamination and they had health problems they would be moved. The crowd calmed down considerably. A little patience was the answer.

Some people still were worried. They said it was too late for them, and for their children. Many feared the future. The man who cried at the first meeting was crying again. It was strange to see a man cry. I never saw a man cry before then. He had one child with a birth defect. He kept on saying, "They're buying my house. Big deal. It's too late. She's already pregnant." He seemed to feel so helpless. I know the governor was trying to do something, but I wondered if he truly understood. So many government officials knew about this for so long and hadn't done anything. That man believed that if they had done something two years ago, he wouldn't have a child with a birth defect and wouldn't be worried sick for his pregnant wife.

After the meeting, Wayne told me to go out in the parking lot and mingle with the residents. But I had to push myself to do anything. The last thing I wanted to do just then was talk to people. I was tired and wanted to go home. But I went and talked to them. Someone tried to sell me some vegetables from his garden. I don't know whether he was kidding. But really, I was feeling pleased with what we had accomplished. Some people were going to be relocated, and the health department was going to study the area outside of rings one and two. And we had a promise that if anything else were wrong, the state would move more people.

2

THE SWALE THEORY

A few days later, I received another lesson in dealing with the state and with politicians. It was something Wayne already knew. It was why we needed a strong citizens' organization. When I went up to the school a few days later, the state officials said they weren't going to buy the homes on ring two. They were going to relocate people only from ring one. They tried to tell us the governor didn't say he was going to move people from ring two. We showed them the newspaper articles that said he did, but that didn't do any good. The man in charge said he would only relocate people in ring-one homes and that was all until he had further orders.

That night we had a meeting with some of Wayne's friends. He had asked them to come because they had experience in protesting and picketing. It seemed we had to do something drastic. A couple of them were hippies with long beards that went down to their belt buckles and long hair. I'm basically square. Before, I would never let such persons in my house, and when they came to my door I thought: *Oh, God. Wayne, what are you getting me into now?* I hoped the neighbors didn't see them come in. They were environmentalists from Canada and professional protesters. But they were nice, well-intentioned people. Wayne also brought a girl from the college, who helped us put a newsletter together.

A Meeting at the White House

About 9:30 that night, Bill Wilcox's office called. He wanted me
to attend a meeting in Washington the next afternoon, August 9.
Things were happening too quickly. He told me the flight number.
"I don't have any money at all," I said. "How am I going to pay
for this?" Wayne said I could buy the ticket on his credit card
and reimburse him when they reimbursed me. That was all right,
so I said I would go. We talked about the meeting in Washington
and why they wanted me there.

I got up at 5:30 the next morning to catch a plane in Buffalo
at 7:00. The group hadn't left until 12:30 or 1:00 the morning
before, and I wasn't really awake. At any other time I would have
been really excited to think I was going to Washington to meet all
those VIPs, but not this morning. I was hopeful because I still
had faith in the government. I thought they wanted to help us.
Governor Carey did say they would buy those homes. He did
make those promises. They had set up a task force. Relocation
officers were working day and night. People from the New York
Department of Transportation were handling the relocation; they
called me when they needed something or when they were trying
to locate this or that pregnant woman, or such and such family.
Everything seemed to be going well. I wasn't excited, and I wasn't
angry. Mostly I was sleepy.

Bill Wilcox met me at the airport. I had no idea how to get
to the White House. I had the safety plan to be used while remedial construction was going on at the canal; but it frightened me.
They still didn't know what was in the canal. Explosives? toxic
gases that could be released? Some of the old-timers thought
the army had dumped chemical warfare materials. (The army
later claimed they hadn't dumped anything.) There was no safety
plan for the residents, only the workers; and the plan didn't say
much about them. Men from around Love Canal worked in
chemical plants. One time a man said: "When you hear the
whistle blow, it's already too late." I thought they should evacuate people who lived in the streets surrounding the canal.

Bill Wilcox met me with a government car. We began with
some small talk. Even though I believed he cared, I felt inadequate talking to him. There were these bigwigs, and here I was, a
peon. I didn't feel then that I had a right to do what I was doing.

In the car, I showed Wilcox the safety plan. I told him I
didn't dare show this to the residents. "Look at it. If this ever

got out, it would be devastating. This says the canal could blow up, or that toxic gases could be released. Something must be done for the residents in this safety plan." Wilcox thanked me for not showing the plan to the residents.

After landing, it took about twenty minutes in the morning traffic to get to the White House. When we got there, I started fumbling for my driver's license or some identification because I thought I would need it to get in. We didn't need any identification. I felt like a school kid.

By now, I was excited. Just think: Lois Gibbs goes to the White House. How many people actually go to the White House on business, not as a tourist? And here I was! We went into the Roosevelt Room. The room was gorgeous! It had high ceilings and beautiful paintings, a huge table, and big china ash trays with gold rims and delicately painted flowers. I wondered whether anyone ever put ashes in something so gorgeous.

I was sitting at one end of the room. I didn't know anybody except Commissioner Whalen, Bill Wilcox, and Congressman LaFalce. The commissioner came over to say hello. We shook hands. No, we didn't shake hands. It felt as if he mangled mine. He squeezed it so hard that my rings were embedded into my fingers. I can't remember all the people who were there, or the departments—HUD and UDT and SDQ. I didn't understand what the initials stood for.

A handsome man called the meeting to order. Everything about him was handsome—his hair, his eyes, his long eyelashes. He said he would like an introduction from each person. After awhile, he called on me as the representative from the community in question. He said he would like to know a little more about Lois Gibbs and Love Canal, about the residents there.

I was nervous, but I managed to introduce myself. I said the safety plan was grossly inadequate, that the health and the lives of the residents were at stake, that we had a lot of illness at Love Canal, and finally that I believed more people had to be evacuated. I told them that evacuations were limited to ring one but that I believed ring two should also be evacuated. The people there also had illnesses. Governor Carey had stated that he would relocate those people as well. But somehow, someone had slipped up somewhere, and the officials on the site didn't get the proper order. I was still nervous, and I was stumbling and stuttering; but somehow I got through it.

We met for about an hour and then went across the street to

another building, possibly the Executive Office Building. Congressman LaFalce walked with me. By then I was very, very tired. I could have fallen asleep just sitting there. They talked about finances and budgeting and about each department's responsibility. I was really surprised to see how hard Congressman LaFalce was working for us. Once I saw him in action, I didn't have any doubts about whether he was on our side. He persisted, shouting and pushing government agency representatives.

I didn't understand one word. I didn't even know why I was there. People were talking a language I didn't understand, using initials and talking about finances.

At the end of the meeting, Tom Frey told me the governor had indeed said ring-two homes could be evacuated. They were going to release the news at a press conference. Then it clicked: they were using me to make it look as if the community had some input. They wanted to make it look as if I had had a part in that decision. Actually, I had no part at all.

After the meeting, we held a press conference on the White House steps. The press asked me how I felt, but by that time I could barely talk. I said I was glad the governor saw what needed to be done and was following through on it. Then we went over to LaFalce's office and had another press conference. I was so tired my eyes would hardly stay open. I almost fell asleep in the congressman's deep red leather chair.

After the press conference, Tom Frey and Jeff Sachs said they wanted me to try to head off the rally scheduled for that night. They were upset because people were threatening to go down to the school and rip it apart. I told them I couldn't stop it, that it was their own fault. They should have made the announcement about the ring-two homes *before* the meeting in Washington. I didn't care about winning friends and influencing people; I just wanted to go home and go to sleep. It had been a wasted day, a wasted trip, a waste of money, and a waste of my time.

The Stigma of Love Canal

When it was all over, they took me back to the airport. I had time to get something to eat, and then I got on the plane to go home. Wouldn't you know it, there was a thunderstorm. It was the end of a perfect day! We sat on the runway for an hour and a half. By the time we took off, the Buffalo Airport had closed; they were working on resurfacing the runways at night. Because it was after 11:00, we had to land in Rochester.

In the plane I went over everything in my mind. Why was I there? Then I realized why. *Hey, look! It's up to you to do it. They made you president. It's your responsibility.* I always try to do the best I can when I have responsibility for anything, whether it be a child, a dog, or a piece of furniture. I said to myself: *You can't sit back and shut your mouth, Lois. You aren't the only one they're hurting. They're hurting hundreds of people. You have to get up there and do it, whether you like it or not, whether you have to push yourself or not, whether you stumble or not.* It was something I had to repeat to myself many, many, times. I still do, even to this day.

After we landed, we had to be bused sixty miles to Niagara Falls. A drunk sat next to me. He smelled so bad that I was getting sick. I had so much coffee I was going to float away anyway. He asked me what I was doing in Washington. I said I had been at a meeting at the White House. I was very proud of that. How many people have meetings in the White House? He asked me what I was doing there, and I said, meeting some people about Love Canal. He asked me if I was contagious! At first, I thought he was kidding. "Yes, if you sit next to me," I said, "you'll get some horrible disease. Because I radiate chemicals." That panicked him. "Are you kidding?" he said. "I'm moving. I ain't going to sit next to you." I suppose the booze had something to do with it; but it *was* funny. He didn't get up and move away, but he did try not to get too close. He wouldn't even put his arm on the arm rest. It was funny in a way: my first encounter with the stigma of Love Canal. The notion that the canal was somehow contagious would reappear. I heard more about that later from people who weren't drunk.

When I finally made it home, I sat down at the kitchen table. The next day was Michael's birthday, and I had forgotten it. I never dreamed I would ever forget a child's birthday. They're kids only once. Kathy had made a coffee cake. It was sitting there on the table, supposed to be a birthday cake, and I didn't know it. My stomach was awash in coffee, and I wanted something to eat. So I ate about three quarters of Michael's cake.

The next morning, Michael was in tears. To think I would eat his birthday cake! Kathy said, "I don't believe you did that. I don't believe you ate Michael's birthday cake." I couldn't explain it to anyone. I went to a useless meeting, flew home exhausted after waiting out a thunderstorm, had to ride on a bus from Rochester in the middle of the night next to a drunk; then I went and ate my son's birthday cake, having forgotten to bake a cake for his birthday.

I was angry. I could have cried. It was Michael's birthday, and I didn't have a gift. No cake. Nothing. The year before, I had to call off his birthday because I hurt my foot. I swore I'd have a nice party for him this year.

I did manage a small birthday party, however. I went out to Child World and bought a bunch of toys; but I didn't have time to wrap them. I bought a cake at the bakery and put some candles on it. The party had to be early, because I had an association meeting that night. But I got hung up during the day because of trouble over at Falcon Manor, an apartment development on the military base, where some of the ring-one and ring-two residents were living temporarily.

It was the same kind of trouble I had encountered on the bus. Some of the parents wouldn't let their children play with Love Canal children because the parents were afraid "they were contagious." They wouldn't let their children touch Love Canal furniture because they thought chemicals on the furniture would harm their children. And they were having a hard time because the apartment manager wanted them to follow rigid military rules. I spent the day trying to get things settled. Because people didn't have dryers, they hung their clothes out on lines, and that led to hassles with the military authorities. It was silly, petty stuff; but it was important to people whose lives were so disrupted. Some were still afraid of what the future might bring. They didn't know where they would live permanently. I was trying to help them live something like normal lives in abnormal circumstances.

By the time I got home, it was late afternoon. Rich Lippes and three of his partners had forms for residents spread out on the couch. They were stapling them together. We had an assembly line working. Meanwhile, the phone kept ringing. People wanted to know about the meeting. Reporters called, asking how the relocation was going, how people were reacting. Poor Michael was shoved aside again; he wasn't having much of a birthday party.

By now it was 7 P.M. and we had to be at the meeting by 7:30. Wayne always said our meetings were going to start on time, that we weren't going to be like New York State. So we lit the candles on the cake and quickly sang Happy Birthday. It may have been the only birthday party for a six-year-old that had four attorneys and two doctors as guests. Michael opened his presents and cut the cake; then the adults left for the meeting. I hope Michael will understand and that he will forgive me someday.

Conducting a Meeting

The meeting was an important one for me. I was becoming tougher and more political as I understood better what I had to do. The meeting was held at Griffin Manor. The black people who lived there thought they were being left out of the relocation plans, and we wanted to include them. We were still having problems getting organized; there was friction.

I had never conducted a meeting before, and had no idea what motions were—how they were carried, voted on, or how discussions were conducted. But I was learning, right then and there. It looked as if it might get out of hand. Wayne walked back and forth, telling them all that bickering was unneccessary, that if that was the way they were going to be, then go ahead; but nothing would be accomplished. I was gaining some confidence, but I was still very nervous. I still couldn't believe it was happening to me. It was as though I were looking at myself up there at the front of the hall.

Two officers had resigned. Debbie Cerrillo was elected vice-president; Jean Hasley, secretary. The lawyers helped people fill out applications for the class-action suits. All in all, I was pleased. The meeting had gone pretty much as planned. The organization had held together.

Working with the Task Force

After the meeting, Mrs. Donahue, who lived at Colvin and 97th Street, asked me to help her. There are two odd-shaped lots on that corner. The state would not buy her house because of the way it stood, even though she had a bad backyard, high chemical readings in her home, and health problems. I told her I didn't know if I could help, but that I would try. The next day, I talked to the state people. They said they would evacuate her. It made me feel good. It was an accomplishment. Up to that time,

I hadn't done anything important—or, at least, I didn't feel I had.

The state set up a task force office at the 99th Street School and an office for us as well. The association's office had men's and ladies' rooms, a refrigerator and a stove, and cupboard space. It had once been the teachers' lounge. The state gave us tables, and the Salvation Army loaned us a typewriter. The state also agreed to pay for our telephone lines—a big help, because we never had more than a few thousand dollars in our treasury. We raised money through members' dues, donations, and speaking fees, and some through raffles, rummage sales, and cake bakes. No one was paid; we were all volunteers. The office had another advantage: I could now take the papers out of my kitchen, out of my cupboards, off my beds, and out of all the other rooms in the house. With our own office, we set up housekeeping.

The office was located right across the hall from the Red Cross, the busiest group at the time. They provided vouchers for security payments for apartments for those moving into temporary quarters. Not many people had the two or three months rent people had to pay in advance to get a rental. The Red Cross bought mattresses for people who had had bedrooms in basements and feared their mattresses were contaminated. Can you imagine what it is like to think that the bed you are sleeping on, or that you put your little children to sleep on at night, is poisoning them? Super Duper and Tops provided food baskets for people who were moving. Everybody went to the Red Cross office across the hall and then came to our office. Thus we were able to stay in close contact with everyone who came into the school.

The health department also set up next to the Red Cross, in the same room. They answered questions about where to go and what to do to get blood tests. They had everybody's files, with the results of all the testing. Whenever residents came out of the health department or the Red Cross room, we'd go up to them and say, "Hi. How are you doing? We're here. Can we do anything? Do you need anything? Here's our phone number. Give us a call any time."

Debbie Cerrillo and I manned the office about 99 percent of the time. Marie Pozniak began coming down to the office, and Grace McCoulf was in periodically. Later, Barbara Quimby came in regularly. I didn't know any one of them very well at that time. Eventually, we became a great team. Even though we were in a tough fight, we laughed and joked a lot. You had to. If you didn't, you either cried or you stayed mad all the time.

The state planned to start the remedial construction on August 17. I explained to the state people that if I showed the safety plan to the residents, they might demonstrate and burn things down, or worse. Our men had guns, and some had been in Vietnam or the earlier wars. They knew about explosives, either from the military or because of their jobs. I didn't know if anyone would have done anything, but I heard talk. If they were pushed hard enough, something could happen.

Because I kept after various officials, meetings were held on the construction plan and the safety plan. People attended from Memorial Hospital, the Red Cross, the Salvation Army, ambulance companies, fire companies, disaster control, the city police, and the state police. Some forty agencies and organizations were represented. I didn't know much about what was going on, other than they were deciding who was responsible for what. That was something I couldn't have cared less about. They were still just talking about the workers. I wanted to know what they were going to do for the residents whose lives were being threatened. But no one had an answer for that.

The Government's Working

We had fought for citizen input, and the state and other official agencies wanted me to say the safety plan was OK. I wasn't going to approve it, however, until they did something to take care of the residents as well as the workers, and until they did something to keep poisons from spreading throughout the neighborhood on the trucks that went in and out. Because dioxin can be toxic in a few parts per trillion, I didn't think I was being unreasonable.

We were worried about people's health while they dug up the canal; but, beyond that, we wanted everyone relocated eventually. In particular, we wanted them to evacuate older people and those already with health problems. Governor Carey said that if people had health problems and if they had contamination in their homes, he would relocate them, just as he had the people on rings one and two. There were two things going on: we wanted a good safety plan, and we were trying to prove that people's health problems were caused by contamination and thus get them relocated. The primaries were being held, and the election would be in November. We knew it, and so did the governor and his people.

Cora Hoffman, Governor Carey's liaison, arrived early in August. At first, I thought that was a hopeful sign. One warm

summer evening soon after she arrived, we invited her to our
house. We had held a board of directors meeting. My living room
was filled with people and smoke. Cora Hoffman was both aggres-
sive and defensive. She kept saying: "I didn't put the damn
chemicals there. Why are you being so unreasonable? Why are
you treating me this way? I didn't put the damn chemicals there.
I didn't have anything to do with them. The governor had nothing
to do with it. It isn't his fault." She spoke as if the *victims* of
Love Canal were to blame.

After talking to her awhile, I began thinking about how
bureaucrats work. Mike Cuddy, the on-site coordinator for the
state's task force, was hard-nosed but competent. We pay the
salaries of people like Cora Hoffman and Mike Cuddy. We put
them in office—at least, indirectly. They're supposed to be
working for us. But they were treating us as if we were an incon-
venience or the enemy or small children they didn't have to explain anything to. It was strange. I never thought government
worked like that. I thought that if you had a complaint, you
went to the right person in the government, and if there were a
way to solve the problem or alleviate it, that they would be glad
to do it. I was to learn differently.

Cora Hoffman had no intention of discussing the problem with
us. After she left, we just sat back in amazement, wondering where
she came from and how we could get rid of her.

The state continued testing blood. Before I got involved in
Love Canal, I had all the confidence in the world in the state of
New York. But the way they organized the blood testing was
ridiculous. They had more than 300 people—tiny children, adults,
senior citizens—all sitting in a hot auditorium. Each person took a
number, filled out a form, and waited, sometimes for hours. Then
it would be time to close up, or they'd run out of needles or vials,
or the nurses had to go home. People who had waited four or
five hours still had to come back the next day.

The state's system was disorganized. We wrote a memo
asking that they reorganize the blood testing. We suggested they
do it street by street or in alphabetical order, or by even-numbered
streets and odd-numbered streets—anything except just coming
to the auditorium and waiting. Also, some of the blood tests that
came back abnormal had to be done again because the blood
samples had spoiled.

Can you imagine waiting in line with a three-year-old for a
blood test, watching fifty three-year-olds in front of you crying
because they were afraid, and then your child gets upset even

before he gets there? Then, when it's your turn, they run out of needles; so you have to take the child back the next day, or you have to go to Children's Hospital to get the blood tested because it was done wrong the first time. It was hard to believe New York State was doing this. Come to think of it, the state did very little right. But I shouldn't say that; the department of transportation ran fairly smoothly. I had some complaints, but all in all, it was a good job.

The health department was terrible; everything they did was disorganized. Either the wrong person was there, or no one could answer questions. After seeing the health department in action, I couldn't figure out who was responsible for the health of New Yorkers. The doctor doing laboratory tests to determine what chemicals were in the area was a smart, likable man with excellent credentials; but he shook all over. He had some kind of neurological disease. But the residents who saw him believed the shaking was the result of working with chemicals, which made them even more afraid.

The health department took air and water samples, which they would put in tubes. The tubes would lie around the school. By the time the samples got to Albany, something would have happened to them, and the readings would come out wrong. One resident had astronomical readings the first time; the next, it came back zero. Why? The department didn't have any answer. I later found out that the home showed evidence of dioxin; yet the air readings in the basement were zero.

The state did many things that shouldn't have been done. Once they put some CETA workers on the canal to cut the grass on the north end with power mowers. The residents got upset because the chemicals had surfaced in some places. The mowers could have set them on fire or touched off an explosion. The CETA workers had no safety clothes. The state didn't think about them any more than they thought about us. We yelled and screamed, and finally they ordered it stopped. The next morning at nine, the CETA workers were out there again. Again, we screamed and hollered, and the state ordered it stopped. The next day, they were out again. We had to confront them every single morning. They would agree with us. "Yes, it should be stopped. We'll do it with sickles."

The state's word meant nothing. I used to believe what people in government agencies told me. But here, they told me they were going to do something, and then they didn't do it. I didn't think they would ever do anything like that. Yet every single day, we had to go out and fight. They said things to pacify me. I learned the hard way by that experience and by many others: no matter what they say, if you don't follow through and fight for something, it's not going to be done, because they're not good for their word.

I was invited to speak to a Head Start Parents meeting, to explain the safety plan to people in the housing projects and to parents who had their children bused into the area for Head Start, which was located in the low-income project near the canal. Many Head Start families were white, and the issue turned into a racial one. The people in Griffin Manor said they were ignored because no studies had been made there.

I tried to explain. I was defending the health department, so they attacked me. They said I was as bad as the state, that I had ignored them, that I had no business there. Why was I there! I was never attacked like that. Cora Hoffman, of course, didn't say a word. Later I found out that she had worked to organize a separate black group instead of helping us work together. Before, my greatest fear was that some one would slam a door in my face. Now, here was a whole group yelling at me.

After the meeting, a nice young black girl came up to me. She asked how I could have possibly stayed through the whole meeting. She wouldn't have. There were certain outside parties there who were known to have used a knife or do something drastic when they were angry. She said they were irrational people. Ignorance was one of the best things I had going for me; it had a lot to do with what I did. I didn't know any better; that's why I wasn't afraid.

The state held another informational meeting on the safety plan for the residents—or rather, the lack of one. Doctors Vianna, Robert Huffaker, and Kim were there. Wayne had some tomatoes he had brought me from his garden. He didn't live near the canal. They all came in and introduced themselves and asked how we were doing. They saw the tomatoes and asked whether they were from Love Canal gardens. We told them, "No. They're for the meeting tonight." I advised them not to sit on the stage because we were going to throw tomatoes. We were kidding, but they took it seriously. When we walked into the meeting, we all laughed. The officials were sitting in the front row of the auditorium; no one was on the stage. They even brought the microphone down to the auditorium floor.

The residents had no intention of allowing them to dig up the canal before they had an adequate safety plan. We believed that the only real safety plan was to evacuate the area. The state couldn't persuade us differently, and some of the things they said made it worse. One woman asked Dr. Huffaker if anything would be in the air. Dr. Huffaker, who was the state's on-site safety officer said, "Yes." The woman then asked: "What will it be like? Is it anything that will hurt my children playing outdoors?" He said, "It will smell like hell. It will smell like Hooker. But it won't hurt you."

"Wait a minute," she said. "If there's an odor in the air, and it's going to smell like Hooker, something must be causing it. How do you know it won't hurt my child?" Dr. Huffaker said: "It will definitely smell. There's no doubt about that. But it won't hurt your baby."

If you use common sense, you know that *something* causes a smell. Your children are going to be breathing it. It could affect their lungs or it could be excreted and cause kidney or liver disease. The construction could go on for weeks or months. It had to affect a child. But Dr. Huffaker expected us to believe that it wouldn't.

Buses were supposed to be available to take people out of the area if toxic chemicals were released. Someone asked Dr. Vianna what he would do if toxic gases were released and the alarm sounded. Would he get on the bus? No, he said, he would run like hell. That was no way to build people's confidence. Yet he didn't understand why people were upset.

Dr. Kim said they had an air-testing device to monitor the air. "What does it test?" "How does it do it?" "How is the air analyzed?" "What kind of staff will you have?" "What are the potential dangers?" Nobody had any answers.

It was pretty much like all the other meetings. They offered no answers, no useful information. The residents' confidence was shaken time and again. They didn't trust the safety plan or the construction plan or the health department officials. People were more frustrated when they left than when they arrived.

I heard later that a state health department official having a drink at a bar after the meeting said he was proud of himself because he hadn't said anything, that he had gotten away with giving political answers. That's the New York State health department. It is supposed to protect public health; but here was one of its officials proud of keeping secrets, proud of keeping things from people about matters that affected their lives!

My First Talk Show

A few days later, Wayne and I did our first television show. I had given press interviews and made on-the-spot comments; but I hadn't done a TV show. I was nervous. The people at the TV station told me what I was supposed to do and not do. Wayne was very informal; he was sprawled on the couch, looking rather unprofessional. The producer asked me if "that guy" was going to go on with me. He must have thought Wayne was the janitor, the way he was dressed.

The interview room was about the size of a closet. Three chairs were shoved close together. There was no air conditioning and no windows. Wayne sat on one side of the interviewer and I sat on the other, facing Wayne. Being with Wayne in a situation like this added to my nervousness. I had the feeling that if I said, "OK," he would hold up a finger. When we went on, the interviewer asked me questions. To answer, I had to look across him right in Dr. Hadley's eyes. I was so self-conscious that everything I said seemed to come out wrong. It seemed like a disaster. The only positive thing I remember was that I was never so happy in my life to get out of a place. That was my first experience on television, and I wasn't so sure I ever wanted to go back.

"They're Working on It"

Three families outside of rings one and two, with poor health records and whose homes were contaminated, were temporarily relocated by United Way. Sixteen more families whose members had various illnesses and whose homes had contaminated air, had submitted complete records to the health department, but they were still living in their own homes. I thought the three families had been moved because of the governor's promise that he would take care of families with health problems and contamination in their homes. I was to find out otherwise.

The three families—Marie Pozniak's, with a very severely asthmatic child; the Grenzys (Mrs. Grenzy was in the first trimester of a pregnancy); and Jim Starr, who had various medical problems—had been relocated temporarily in a downtown hotel.

United Way paid for everything. Each family had letters from doctors, stating that they should be relocated because the digging might aggravate their health problems. Joe Maloney, of United Way, agreed to cover the costs with money from a special fund. The State of New York promised to review its records to determine whether to relocate them permanently and buy their homes or return them to their homes after construction was complete.

The families moved to the hotels, even though it wasn't easy for them. Marie Pozniak was working in the Homeowners Association office full time. Mrs. Grenzy was worried—about her home, her pregnancy, and her other two children. While in the hotel, her husband also became ill. I was afraid that, between her fears and the chemicals, she would have a miscarriage. I called every day to check.

Dr. Vianna told me that all the families in the same situation (with health problems and contaminated homes) should submit records from their private physicians. They should also fill out forms, have blood samples taken, and submit everything to Albany for a relocation review. Residents' morale was lifted. People were finally ready to believe there was a way out for them, just as there had been for the people in the first two rings around the canal. Still naive, we believed almost everything we were told. Although we fought state officials about other things, nothing else was as important as this. Although they had lied to us before, we never stopped to think about that. We had faith in the State of New York. We believed everything they said. People followed the rules. All the consent forms were filled out. We checked with the health department. If the doctors hadn't sent the records, we had the residents call their doctors. The health department seemed to cooperate. They sent someone to visit the slower doctors and helped with photocopying records. Happy the review had started, we anxiously awaited the results. Joe Maloney, of United Way, kept calling about the expense of maintaining the three families in hotel rooms.

We wanted the governor to come for another meeting. By now we had quite a large agenda. The governor said he couldn't come; but Tom Frey, his aide, and Commissioner Whalen came. They wanted to know what the problems were. Wayne Hadley, Matt Murphy, Debbie Cerrillo, and some other members of the board of directors and I told them what was happening and what we wanted. Tom Frey said he would take it back to the governor and get back to us. We wanted the same help they provided for

ring-one and ring-two houses. We were asking for help in getting
out of the area and in protecting property values for those who
wanted to stay. By now our homes were worthless. Real-estate
agents wouldn't even list Love Canal homes.

After the meeting, Commissioner Whalen went over to
Griffin Manor. He poked his head in a few basements and told
people the smells came from a sewer, that it had nothing to do
with Love Canal. That seemed like an irresponsible thing for a
health commissioner to do. If I had done that, people would have
said, "You can't do that. You don't have data. You didn't do
air readings. You didn't have them analyzed. You need to do it
for twenty-four hours or forty-eight hours." But the health commissioner can go over there and use his nose.

The health department doctors on site changed every couple
of weeks. There were at least five of them. I don't know whether
the health department did it to confuse the residents or because
their personnel couldn't tolerate the strain. Those personnel were
the key to our release; therefore, they were attacked the most
often. Having been attacked myself, I can feel for them, but they
caused a lot of their own troubles.

"Dr. Four" would just sit there and smile and never say a word.
At one point, I wasn't sure whether he was alive. He just nodded
his head up and down, and up and down. I asked him if there was
something wrong with one woman's blood. Eight months pregnant, she had an extremely high alkaline phosphate level. He
shook his head up and down, up and down. I said, "What should
she do about it?" He shrugged his shoulders. I asked him if he
could do anything, and he shook his head, no. "What about her
family physician?" I asked. Finally, he said something. "Yes,
that's who you go to, your family physician." I asked him again:
What should she do? Again, he shrugged his shoulders.

"Dr. Three" may be a very intelligent man, but he had no
common sense, nor any sense of how to deal with the residents. He
just didn't know how to talk to them or even approach them. A
resident would say, "I've got a reading in my basement." Dr.
Three would tell them there was no problem there. He would say,
"Look at Los Angeles air." Someone else would come in with an
abnormal blood test or liver test, and he would say: "You have
a problem in your blood, but it's probably because you're smoking
so much or because you drink." He had an answer for everything.
He just couldn't talk to the residents, couldn't relate to them or
understand them. A lot of the residents hated the man.

The health department wasn't the only less-than-helpful agency. Except for a few people who were working on their own —like Dr. Vincent Ebert, a geographer, Dr. Paigen, and Addie Levine, a sociologist—we didn't get any help from the State University of New York (SUNY) at Buffalo either. We had many technical questions about the construction, the testing procedures, and the ways chemicals could disperse through an area.

The president of the SUNY at Buffalo said he would set up a university task force. They were going to have a meeting of the steering committee, and sent me a letter saying they were setting it up. But to this day, that's all they ever sent me. Dr. Levine said the task force was trying to identify the problems they would work on. I gave her some questions that were important to us and I asked her to ask the university task force about the permeability of soil. She passed the questions along, but I never heard from the university task force. I have since learned that they put together a library of newspaper clippings.

SUNY is another state bureaucracy. By rights, it should be serving the public; but some professors were worried because their grants came from the health department. Some didn't want to get mixed up in anything that could go to court. Some without tenure were simply afraid of everything. It was a shame; everybody could have benefited. We could have been a laboratory for a lot of fields, such as medicine, psychology, botany, and toxicology.

The health department had been promising us the results of the relocation reviews in a week; then it was another week and another, and we hadn't yet heard anything. United Way was running out of money. Dr. Glenn Haughie, the health department's deputy commissioner, said they were working on it, that they had to evaluate everything carefully. But they didn't have complete records. Doctor Vianna was supposed to call me every day, to tell me whose records were incomplete and what they needed. I could always go to an individual or to a family, if I knew what was needed. They also told us they would have the results for the completed records they did have in a few more days.

I told Dr. Haughie that the families in the hotel were going to be thrown out first thing the next morning because United Way had used up its special fund. Transportation commissioner William Hennessy, who was chairing the intergovernmental task force, said he would see what he could do. I thought: *Great. So he could find funds so the families can be put up for a few more days.* But then, it was getting confusing. At first, state officials said they moved people because of health problems. Maybe they did it because the governor was campaigning. Then, a day later, they said the moves were because of the remedial construction on the canal. State and federal agencies were fighting about who was going to pay for what; so the state just changed what they said because they thought it would help in getting federal money. It made me angry. We were talking about people's lives, and they were playing political and bureaucratic games.

We kept asking for a control-group study. We were repeatedly promised one, but they haven't done one to this day. Dr. Haughie said at a meeting that 25 percent of all people die from cancer. How do we know how much cancer we have at Love Canal? The health department couldn't tell without a control group; so why haven't they done controlled studies?

We also asked them to call in the National Institute of Environmental Health Sciences (NIEHS). This is a curious subject. The health department kept saying they had asked NIEHS time and again, but had never received a reply. Someone I know at the National Institute said they were never invited. A year later, I discovered the state health department and NIEHS were still playing bureaucratic games.

Mayor O'Laughlin headed up a future-land-use committee, but he was never on our side. "Let's get it over with. You are hurting Niagara Falls with your publicity. There is no problem here." He still doesn't think there's a problem, except, perhaps, for rings one and two, and that's only because Commissioner Whalen's order of August 2, 1978, forced the city to do something about cleaning up the canal. Until then, the city, Hooker, and the board of education had been having meetings; but no one did anything. For all the city cared, they could have swept the whole thing under a rug.

In the early fall, Governor Carey came to Love Canal and spent about an hour there. Mike Cuddy called to tell us he was coming. Could I meet him at the school? Mike told me the press had been notified; to make sure, I called all of the newspapers and TV stations myself. We knew the TV and newspaper reporters were our friends, and I was doing everything I could to help them.

I had already met Governor Carey a couple of times. By now, I felt less intimidated. Debbie Cerrillo sat next to me. That gave me some courage. I knew that if I flubbed, Debbie would take over. Wayne was there, but he didn't go into the meeting with the governor. Wayne didn't want to come in because he was leaving soon, and he wanted me to handle things on my own.

I brought up the subject of the control group, the safety plan for the residents, and the people who needed to be moved from the hotel. I kept telling the governor he had promised at the beginning of August that if there were health problems or contamination, he would relocate us. People were living in a hotel, with their expenses paid by United Way, and everyone from the State of New York seemed to be ignoring them. Why? Well, he said, if we find contamination, and if they have related health problems, we will not ignore them. I said, "Excuse me, sir. Are you going to relocate these people if you find contamination in their homes and they have health problems?" He just repeated what he said, "If there are health problems. . . ."

He sounded as if he were promising, but I tried to pin him down. He used tricky language. He said things that sounded as if they meant one thing, but when you came down to it, he could say he didn't say that at all. He was very careful in front of the newspapers and the television cameras. I made my mistake in not asking the governor *who* would take care of them. It turned out that he meant United Way or some other voluntary agency, welfare or whatever; not the State of New York, and not the assistance they had provided for rings one and two.

I was excited. I still had the naive belief that the governor meant what he said. And if anything is naive, it is the belief that government officials and politicians will do what they say they will do. I was so excited, I didn't bother to wait for Governor Carey's statement to the press. I should have; then I could have confronted him in front of the press if he changed his statement. Wayne thought I should have stayed and pressed him to say it on TV, in that thirty seconds when the press would ask him what he was going to do.

I ran down the hall to tell everybody what I thought the governor had said—if you have contamination, and if you have illnesses, you will be relocated. "It came from the governor. He can't back out of it." Boy, was I wrong! He twisted it to the point where *no one* could qualify for relocation. He said that the residents had to *prove* their health problems were caused by Love Canal. How can anyone prove the canal caused a particular illness? Everyone knows you can't prove that in every case. That's what he said in the press release, and I didn't realize it until after he had left. There I was, running down the hall all excited, hoping that when the health review was completed, the residents would be moved.

Discovery of the Swale Theory

At the end of September, Dr. Vianna brought in a team to do a health survey outside rings one and two. He asked me to help. I still believed that he wanted to help us, that he was looking out for the people, and not just doing studies.

I sent flyers to all the residents, asking them to cooperate. The flyers asked them to report their illnesses and get their doctors' records to Dr. Vianna. Street representatives took the flyers door-to-door. By now, we were well organized, with representatives on every street.

Many residents talked with Dr. Vianna. He was always very nice to them. When I asked him about Love Canal, he said that if you closed your eyes and went to Rutherford, New Jersey, you could smell the same things you smelled in Niagara Falls. As far as he was concerned, the whole city of Niagara Falls was contaminated, not just the Love Canal area. There was no way to prove that illnesses were *not* caused by other contamination, and not just Love Canal. Of course, that was why we needed a good control group. At that time, he seemed our best hope. I decided to work with him and see what we could do.

The women in the Homeowners Association office called to make sure people would be home to fill out the health survey, and to ask them to cooperate. We didn't take a survey ourselves. When people said they had a health problem, though, we wrote it down.

I had just come home from a meeting with Wayne. It was nearly two in the morning. Although I was tired, I kept thinking there must be a way to prove the illnesses were caused by the canal. I took out our health-survey notebook and started to put squares, triangles, and stars on a street map, with a different symbol for each disease group: central-nervous-system problems, including hyperactivity, migraines, and epilepsy; birth defects and miscarriages; and respiratory disorders. Suddenly a pattern emerged!

I knew of one swale, an old stream bed that went behind my house. I drew that swale on the map. Later, I drew a swale that

Art Tracy, Mary Richwalter, and some of the other old-time residents had told me about. Actually, my neighbors drew the line for the swales. I was surprised: the illnesses clustered along the swales. I had very little data at this time, but the central-nervous-system and neurological problems, the migraines, epilepsy, and hyperactivity followed the swale. The birth defects made a perfectly straight line parallel to Frontier Avenue. The birth defects were in houses that stood back to back. It looked like every house on a corner or near one had a child with a birth defect. Houses at the north end of the canal had respiratory problems. That surprised me. I kept looking at it and looking at it, rechecking to make sure I had done it right. It was right. All the illnesses were there.

The next morning, I photocopied the map with my discovery. Marie looked it over and added a few more homes with illnesses. When Dr. Vianna came in, I said: "Look. I put the illnesses on the map with stars, triangles, and squares—and look what I came up with." He looked at it but didn't say much. Then he asked: "What is it?" I explained that it was clusters of illnesses along old stream beds and in swampy areas. Residents on the south end said it had always been swampy there. I came to the conclusion that the respiratory problems were to the north because of the way the wind blew. The wind comes off the river and is fresh at the south end of the canal. Then, as it crosses the canal, it must pick up contamination from the surface of the canal, and the central and northern portions get it.

Dr. Vianna looked at the map curiously. He said he would follow up on it, but he wasn't sure there was much to the theory. If I could get verification as to where the swales were, and the wet areas, he would put it in the computer along with the medical data. I had confidence that Dr. Vianna was going to do it scientifically.

I also showed the map to Mike Brown of the Niagara Falls *Gazette*, and he published it. As a result of his article, more people called to tell me where swampy places were and where diseases were.

Then I called Dr. Paigen. She suggested we do a full survey of illnesses along the swales and swampy areas. She also told me to have people tell us exactly what illnesses they had and whether they had been to the doctor for diagnosis. The following day, we started our own medical survey.

We had never done a survey before. None of us knew how to

approach people. We were supposed to ask, "Do you have epilepsy? Do you have migraines? Have you had a nervous breakdown? Did somebody in your family ever attempt suicide?" People don't easily talk about things like that. Also, I didn't know the right questions. We started out asking very general questions: "Do you have any health problems?" If they said, "Yes, respiratory," we wrote down respiratory instead of bronchitis or asthma, unless they specified it. Dr. Paigen supervised our survey. We called some people several times to get everything we needed. We asked how long they had lived there, how many children they had, and how many adults lived in the house. We needed a complete population count. We found out their places of employment; whether they worked at Hooker or some other chemical plant, and if they did, whether they worked in the plant or the office. We had to call back several times as we learned the hard way what questions it was most important to ask.

Some of the residents were frustrated and uncooperative. They believed we were blowing the Love Canal problem all out of proportion. Just go away, lady! Fortunately, only a few families refused to cooperate. We completed our health survey with enough data to permit a careful analysis. Dr. Paigen helped us every step of the way. A highly respected scientist, she helped with the tables and statistics and in interpreting the results. She had enough confidence in what we did to go out on a limb.

While we did our study, residents outside the first two rings were receiving their air readings. One woman on 102d Street had a positive air reading in her basement. She asked the health department what she should do. They said her reading was high, and told her not to stay in the basement. "Just throw the laundry in and come right back up. Don't spend any time down there." Two people in that house had epilepsy and two had asthma. She had gynecological problems. I don't know how they expected her to feel. Did they think it would make her feel safer when they told her not to use the basement in her own home?

Later she received readings for her son's bedroom. They came out very close to the ones in the basement. Now she couldn't go in the basement *or* her son's bedroom. What was she to do with her children? Her son's bedroom door opened into the living room. The contamination could spread to every room. Where could she go? She was angry and afraid. She didn't want to leave her children in the house any longer, but she had no relatives nearby. Who could take her children? Besides, she was worried about the potential psychological damage in sending her children to live away from their parents.

Her basement flooded just about daily and smelled like Hooker Chemical on a bad day. The basement readings indicated one of the isomers of lindane, a deadly pesticide. She had a coliform reading (an intestinal bacteria count) that went off the top of the scale. Yet, she had to continue to live in that house.

After we completed the health survey, we put the air readings in the houses on the map to see if the air readings correlated to the spread of illnesses. Debbie and I collected as many air readings as we could. There seemed to be very low levels of chemicals in the air readings of houses on 99th Street right across from the school, especially compared with north and south of that area. We couldn't figure out why.

Incidentally, the school doesn't have a basement. When they started digging a foundation, the contractor ran into the chemicals. The engineers told the school board they couldn't put a basement there because of corrosive chemicals. The school board told the engineers to build the school a few yards away from the canal and put it on a slab. They knew what they were doing, but it didn't seem to make any difference to them.

Eventually we found out why the air readings were so low. The school board had had a French drain installed around the school, which collected the contaminated leachate and diverted it into the storm sewers, from which it passed eventually into the Niagara River. It's ironic. I would laugh if it weren't so tragic. The school board and the city knew what was in the canal and what kind of poisons were going into the Niagara River; but they blamed us for ruining Niagara Falls with bad publicity!

The air readings and illnesses didn't show any correlation. Dr. Paigen went over it and said it didn't make sense. There were more than 200 chemicals in the canal, but the air readings detected only eight. If you stop to think about the difficulties in doing the studies, you can see why we were feeling so down about getting proof. They kept telling us that there was no proof. But not being able to prove a relationship because it is impossible to do the studies is not the same as proving the chemicals don't have anything to do with people's diseases—which seems to be what the state was saying. Besides, I don't see why you need scientific certainty when people's lives and health are at risk. Even though we couldn't show the relationship, the swales study proved to be important later on, when we finished it.

Remedial Work

The remedial work on the canal was supposed to begin October 10. Buses were to evacuate people in the event of an explosion or the release of gases. At the last task force meeting, they agreed to a dry run, so we would know whether people could get out, the people would know what to do, and the bus drivers would know where to go. I said I wanted the residents to participate, but they were very hesitant. Eventually they agreed. To my mind, without that, it would be like having a school fire drill without the children leaving the building.

Press coverage for the evacuation drill was heavier than usual; there must have been twenty reporters and several TV cameras. The buses went from street to street, but many of them didn't stop to pick up our people. Grace McCoulf stood on the corner of Colvin and 102d Street with her two children. Seven buses passed her by. As a matter of fact, one bus driver who knew her waved at her. Grace called and said, "Aren't they supposed to pick people up?" "Yes," I said. She replied: "Well, I'm dead by now." I asked the news reporter to take pictures of Grace, her two children, and her baby-sitter sitting on the curb at the corner next to the evacuation sign waiting to be picked up. The media had a grand time with that government goof.

October 10 was D day, the day they were supposed to begin construction. Actually, it was just a media event. The equipment drove on-site and the workers dug a ceremonial hole for the television cameras. Steve Lester, our toxicologist, arrived that day. The state had agreed to pay for our on-site expert, to ensure that all the safety precautions were being followed. It was a busy day, what with all the news reporters. I gave Steve what little data I could find that day.

In the midst of all this, a street representative from north of Colvin arrived and asked if he could talk to me privately. He was upset, and I was thinking: *What's he going to blast me for now?* Not everybody was happy about the construction or the safety plans. We went into the other room, and he started crying. I didn't know what to say or do. I sat there waiting for him to compose himself. His neighbor's seven-year-old boy had just died. This representative believed the child's death was related to Love Canal. He was still crying. I thought: *Oh, God, isn't this ever going to end? Everyone who comes in here is crying about something that breaks your heart just to hear it.* This little boy had been playing baseball and football. He showed no sign of illness. All of a sudden, his body swelled up. He was hospitalized twice, and then he died. He had apparently been a healthy, normal child. The man, who had been close to the boy, sat there and cried his eyes out.

Dr. Paigen and the child's mother wanted an autopsy, to determine whether there were toxic chemicals in his liver, kidneys, or other tissues. The health department did do an autopsy. There were many unusual findings for his condition (nephrosis), but the department did nothing about the autopsy results. Months later, at a public meeting with the health department, the child's mother Luella Kenny said she had read in a newspaper that the health department had finished its investigation, but that they had never told her. Dr. Axelrod, who was present, apologized, saying it was an oversight. Luella, who had the full support of her husband Norman, became very active in the Homeowners Association. She is a very effective speaker. She even went to a stockholders' meeting of Occidental Petroleum, Hooker's parent company. The stockholders' meeting was held on the birthday of the board chairman, Dr. Armand Hammer. They listened to her politely and then went on with the board meeting and birthday celebration.

Sitting there watching that man cry gave me one of the worst, most helpless feelings I had had in all this. The federal government was feuding with the State of New York, when they could have been relocating people and this little boy might have been saved. If he had been moved from the canal area, perhaps he would not have died. On the other hand, maybe it would have made no difference. I don't know. It went around and around in my mind. What do you tell a man who is crying over the death of a neighbor's child and is thinking that his little boy could be next? It shook me, too. Michael had had some symptoms similar to the ones that little boy had. I tried to reassure the man that we would keep trying; but there were no words to express my real sorrow. You can only listen and hope it helps someone to talk it out.

One day just as we were closing the office, a man came in. No one noticed him at first because we were watching the news on TV. He lived on 97th Street, on ring one. The state was going to move him. The man stood there weeping. I had never seen so many men crying. It takes a lot to make a man cry, and this was the fourth or fifth man I had seen recently with tears in his eyes. The men in our neighborhood don't cry. They are he-men, the type of men who protect their families and will let nothing hurt them. To see so many men cry really upset me.

He said that somebody had to help him. He was watching the early news, showing the start of construction. As he was watching it, a bulldozer knocked down his own garage, just pushed it down. All his tools were there, as well as other things he had saved for years to buy. They tossed his pool filter to one side and bowled over his pool. He was upset because it was still his house. Although the state said they would buy his house and he intended to sell, he hadn't yet signed any papers. It was still his house, and it was still his garage. He had been watching the TV news, and unexpectedly he was watching his garage and pool being destroyed. No one had told him it was going to happen.

An older man, he and his wife lived by themselves. I don't know if they had grown children who lived away, but his house meant a great deal to him. It was still his home, yet someone had broken into the garage, taken everything out and tossed it to one side, had broken into the house and turned the electricity off. Then they had bulldozed the garage. He was trembling, he was so upset.

I took him across the hall to the Department of Transportation office. I thought he was going to slug Mike Cuddy, but that wasn't why I took him. Mike said he was sorry, that they shouldn't have done that without first buying his property, and that they would make amends. They would pay him for the garage and anything that was damaged. But the man just stood there, silent, getting madder and madder. Clearly, he didn't believe Mike. Did the man ever get the money? I don't know, but I do know I'll never forget him standing there furious and helpless, with tears in his eyes. How would you like to see your house bulldozed down as you're watching on television? All his life's savings, all his hard work, all the love he put into his house and no one bothered to tell him. It is hard to imagine what that's like, but in one way or another everyone who had to leave, everyone whose home had been destroyed, felt the same way.

Relocation Denied—The State Lying Again

We were still working on our health survey. Dr. Vianna kept promising that he would check our findings, but he hadn't as yet done anything. He also promised that we would receive word about whether the three families living in the hotels would be relocated. We waited until 10:00 on the morning of the day he named. When we hadn't heard anything, I called him. Naturally, he was in a meeting. Then I called Commissioner Whalen, who said the decision had already been made, that the response would come special delivery. I asked, "Why not just call up the people and tell them what the decision is?" He said that's not the way they do it, that it was in the mail, and we would receive it fairly soon. I reminded him that the residents had to be out by ten the next morning. United Way had run out of funds. He refused to tell us his decision over the phone. The residents would have to wait, and that's all there was to it. Maybe it would arrive later that afternoon.

I didn't want Marie or any of the other residents to find out without me being there, if nothing else so we could laugh and celebrate together. More likely, it would be to cry together. The situation didn't look good. If the answer was yes, he would have told me, so it had to be no. The residents had been waiting since August. United Way officials were upset. The residents were upset. Some of them couldn't eat or sleep. Many just sat there and cried. It was all red tape. The decision had been made.

Nothing came that night, although some of the residents waited up until midnight. The next morning, there were many news reporters at the office. I called Whalen's office and told them the response hadn't arrived. The residents had to check out of the hotel. They were sitting in their cars wondering what to do. Whalen said they would receive the written notice by noon. If they didn't, he would make a verbal statement. Soon afterward, one of the news reporters called Whalen. Commissioner Whalen told him the decision within thirty seconds of the time I hung up! All the families had been denied relocation. It was unbelievable. That, on top of the fact that the decision had been given to a news reporter first!

I called Grace McCoulf. "Grace, go over and sit with Marie, because the response is negative." I called Patti Grenzy's husband and told him he better be with her because she wasn't going to be happy about the news. She was already very nervous.

When the news came, many of the residents cried. They didn't know what to do or say. Some were furious because they had received identical form letters when they were told that each would be evaluated individually. It wasn't so much being refused; they were all refused relocation because the canal wasn't going to

blow up! We thought the review was to be of construction-related
health problems because of the chemical readings where we lived,
not whether the canal would blow up. They assured us that every
family's health problems would be reviewed individually. The
health department didn't believe it was necessary to relocate
people at this time.

I called Deputy Commissioner Haughie. "There is no appeal,"
he said. I called Vianna and angrily asked him what he was doing.
What kind of review was this? I called Senator Moynihan's aide. I
called Dr. Five the current DOH physician on site. I called everyone I could think of: Commissioner Hennessy, Matt Murphy,
Governor Carey. I even called Duryea, who was running against
Carey. I called the news reporters and the TV people.

The nineteen families that were supposedly reviewed were
desolate when they came into the Homeowners Association office.
Many felt they had lost their last chance to get out. Marie was
crying. When her daughter had been living away from the Love
Canal house, she didn't need any medication. She hadn't been ill.
This child was a severe asthmatic who took medicine regularly.
Marie couldn't bring that child back, but she had no choice. Patti
Grenzy was pregnant. Kathy Aul had come out of the hospital
with her baby that very morning. A few people had cancer, and
they were afraid it would spread faster because of the chemicals.
People didn't know what to do or where to go from here. There
was no appeal. The tension was powerful—people crying, throwing their hands up, pacing back and forth, walking up and down
staircases, just not knowing what to do. Although the media gave
it a lot of space, we were back to day one.

More than anything else, this incident convinced me we
would have to fight for our interests—and our lives. The state had
lied to us. We believed them when they said they would help us.
Governor Carey said people with health problems, whose houses
were contaminated, would be relocated; but the health department made the decision, based on how safe it was to dig in the
canal. We had been toyed with until we agreed to the safety plan,
until they turned that first spade of earth. Then they told us, in
effect, that they never had any intention of helping us. Some of
the residents couldn't handle the disappointment; one or two
were talking about suicide, and not idly, either. They were deadly
serious. And New York State had no feelings for them. The state
didn't want to spend the money, and that's all there was to it.

I felt I had to do something, after being with the nineteen

families refused relocation. I called the child-abuse hot line in Albany and demanded that Commissioner Whalen be arrested for child abuse. I was quite serious. I called the hot line and said I would like to report a case of child abuse. Hundreds of children were being abused. A child in the area had died. I wanted to press charges against Commissioner Whalen, New York State's health commissioner. The man at the other end of the line didn't know what to do with me. He knew who I was. He knew about Love Canal. And he knew who Commissioner Whalen was. He turned me over to his supervisor. I said to the supervisor: "I would like to press charges against Commissioner Whalen. He is subjecting children to toxic chemicals that are adversely affecting their health. One child died recently. We don't want more children to die, but he refuses to relocate them or to recommend relocation." The supervisor decided he couldn't handle the situation, and turned me over to *his* supervisor. I went up the line through seven supervisors. They finally concluded that I couldn't place child-abuse charges against Commissioner Whalen. He was a civil servant, doing his duty.

Then I tried to call Secretary of Health, Education, and Welfare, Joseph Califano, but I couldn't get through to him. He was never around, or he was always in a meeting. I talked to someone else though. I said that getting us out of the Love Canal area was a matter of our health and our welfare, and within the jurisdiction of his department. The man said I would have to talk to the Environmental Protection Agency. By now I knew what the initials "EPA" meant. I told him the EPA wasn't doing anything. It had put up a small amount of money to repair the canal but had nothing to do with health studies. We needed someone to protect the health and welfare of our children. But he just gave me the runaround; there was nothing he could do, he said. I was beginning to learn how fragmented the federal government is, how far removed the top people are, protected by secretaries, regulations, and paper from contact with ordinary people.

Fighting Back

Although we were frustrated, I made many good friends as a result of Love Canal. You couldn't ask for better friends to work with than Debbie, Grace, and Marie. There were many others, too. I invited everyone for a wine-and-cheese party to plan our next move. We had a great time, laughing, joking, enjoying being together. We thought about a bus to Albany but dropped the idea when we found out it would cost six to eight hundred dollars.

We had to do something. Since Albany was out because of the cost, we decided to hold our protest at Niagara Falls City Hall in the hope that Mayor O'Laughlin would call or write to the governor or someone in the federal government in support of the Love Canal residents. We hoped his intervention would result in a declaration that we lived in a disaster area so we could get support in relocating. About fifty people went to City Hall, a large crowd for a working day. The mayor wasn't in; he was speaking at LaSalle High School. We went over there. A toddler, a little girl about two and a half, went up to him and stuck her forefinger out, pointed at him, and said: "Mayor Locklin, what are you going to do for me?" It was cute, and the media picked it up. We always saw to it that our protests had coverage, because that was really the only thing we had going for us. The mayor said he would write a letter. If he did, I never saw it; and I asked him for a copy many times. The children in the school received an unexpected lesson in political reality, a lesson that I feel is important, because I knew nothing about it before Love Canal. I wish I had.

The Phil Donahue Show

Phil Donahue wanted us on his show. Debbie was so excited. She ran up and down the hall: "Phil Donahue is going to have us on TV! Phil Donahue is going to have us on TV!" It *was* exciting —and important—but I felt cool about it. A year earlier I would have been thrilled to say I was going to be on Phil Donahue's show. I would have been excited and nervous. Just before I did the show I was nervous, but hearing about it didn't do for me what it did for Debbie. I wondered whether it would do anything to help get the residents out of there. That was uppermost in my mind.

Donahue's assistant said I could bring two other residents. When I told the assistant about the swale theory and the map, she said bring it along; maybe they could use it on the show. We weren't going to be featured. They wanted us on the show with a Dr. Samuel Epstein who had written a book about the environment and cancer. I had never heard of him or his book, but if I could tell people about Love Canal, it would be worth it. I told my mother, who was as excited as, if not more so than, Debbie.

I thought about the opportunity the Phil Donahue show provided to blast Governor Carey on national TV. Practically every housewife in the country watches Phil Donahue. I had when I was a full-time housewife. Because I had always been honest with Commissioner Hennessy, I told him I had every intention of blasting Governor Carey on television. Then we would see if he got reelected. I told Hennessy I was a housewife and that housewives watch Phil Donahue, and that those housewives vote. I also dropped the threat in a newspaper interview. I wanted to see what effect it would have. I gave Rich Lippes my phone number in Chicago in case he heard anything. Commissioner Hennessy called Rich the night before and told him the governor would not be threatened. If I went on television, so be it; but that would not intimidate the governor. Actually, I didn't get much of a chance to say anything on the Phil Donahue show. I regret now that I didn't seize the opportunity.

We flew to Chicago for the show. It was the first time Marie Pozniak had ever flown. We took a taxi to the gorgeous Hyatt Regency. A year ago, I never imagined I would be in a place like this, with huge chandeliers, a doorman, and bellboys. Debbie was funny about the bellboy. She wouldn't let go of her suitcase. I kept telling her it was a high-class place, that people there don't steal suitcases. But still she held on. She wouldn't let go. The bellboy who took her bag from the taxi put it against a wall. She grabbed it back and clung to it.

We were all innocent then. Debbie has since changed considerably. Today, even though she was on ring one and was relocated, she is one of the most effective association workers. Debbie has spoken to groups all over, and she can really move a crowd of people. Because of her, there's a town in New Jersey that isn't going to become another Love Canal. She told them what had really gone on at the canal and had the whole audience crying. When she finished, those people were definitely not going to allow a "scientifically safe" toxic chemical waste dump to be built next to their high school, as a certain company wanted to do and the town wanted to let the company do.

Our rooms were on floors twenty-six, twenty-seven, and twenty-eight. What were we going to do on three different floors? We stopped in each room to see which was the best. Mine was a suite, with a little conference room and table, a king-size bed, and a couch. Debbie and Marie had twin-bed rooms. They decided to sleep in my room, mainly because Debbie didn't like to sleep alone. I told them, *No way*. I wanted at least one night's sleep without the press or anyone else calling and without people sleeping all over the floor. Reluctantly, they slept in one of their rooms.

That evening we walked around the hotel. We were fascinated, never having been in a place like that before. We went into the bar. Some men tried to, I guess you would call it, "make" us. I don't know what they call it nowadays. Anyway, it was kind of fun. It had been a long time since we had done anything like that, and we had a good time.

The next morning we took a taxi to the studio. As we were sitting in the waiting room, right down the hall, we could see Bozo the Clown with a bunch of kids. On the way down the hall, we went past other shows in progress in studios on either side of the hall. Phil Donahue's studio was nothing like what I had imagined. I'd assumed there were a hundred or so people in the audience, but there were only twenty-five or thirty. I thought it would be like a theater, but there were folding chairs.

We were thrilled to be there, anyway. Donahue shook hands and took us into a small room to brief us. He wanted his show lively with audience participation. Keep the conversation going. If we didn't agree with what he, Donahue, said, argue with him. We sat on one side; Dr. Epstein was on the stage. He had an old man with him who could barely make it up the hall. They talked about Dr. Epstein's book, *The Politics of Cancer*. The older man described how he had been poisoned and stated that industry knew about it.

They finally called me up. I didn't know what it was all about. I wasn't familiar with television at all. No one understood ring one and ring two. To them, that was a local matter. I mentioned the health problems, the miscarriages, and the birth defects. Then Dr. Epstein took over. He wouldn't let me back in. I was upset. It was my inexperience more than anything else, I think; if I'd had another chance, he wouldn't get away with that.

Marie, Debbie and I were unhappy about the whole experience. The show didn't air for two weeks, so we had plenty of time to prepare our relatives and friends for what could only be a major disappointment.

Housewife's Data

Everything was a struggle. The New York State Health Department didn't want to meet with us on our health survey data. The Niagara County Medical Society was concerned about the health department interfering with private doctors, and many doctors weren't cooperating in getting out the health data.

Even the board of education gave us a hard time. Many of our children went to the 93d Street School. They used to be able to walk home for lunch, but we didn't want our children walking past the canal while the construction was going on. We wanted them to have lunch at school. One of the assistant superintendents told us they couldn't serve lunch. When we went to the school board meeting to find out why, we were told that the board members hadn't heard anything about it. The school administrators hadn't brought it up. Eventually the school board hired a lunchroom aide and some bus aides. We convinced them that it would cost the school board more if children were absent from school with a lot of flimsy excuses than if the school put on a few aides. I don't know why they made us fight. Because of the emergency situation, they probably would be reimbursed by the state. All they had to do was fill out an application.

About this time, President Carter came to Buffalo, campaigning with Governor Carey and Senator Moynihan. We decided to meet them with big signs and a big crowd. Senator Moynihan sent word he wanted to meet with me when the others had left. The residents went to the Buffalo Airport, where the politicians were to make an appearance. Many who came to see the President were willing to hold signs for us. The residents spread the signs all through the crowd, so it would look like most of the people there were from the canal. Some of the signs weren't very complimentary of Governor Carey. They called him a murderer or a child abuser and asked why he was discriminating against residents who lived two blocks from the canal. It made good press for us.

Debbie Cerrillo got up close to President Carter. When she tried to tell him about Love Canal, he shook her hand and smiled; but all he said was, "I'll pray for you." That was about all we got from Washington for the next two years.

Afterwards, Senator Moynihan met me in Niagara Falls. While we were talking, we walked out to the center of the canal. Jim Clark and Lee Lutz were there and both were very articulate. Lee had lived there a long time. Black ooze was coming through the basement wall of his house. One wall had moved because of the pressure.

Moynihan has an unusual way of speaking. He kept saying, "Elegant." When we told him he was standing on the canal, he said, "How elegant." All he really said was the basic too-bad-it-happened type of thing. You could look out over the canal from an upper floor in the school. While we were up there, I showed him my swale map. "Look," I said; "there are health problems that are related to the stream beds that carry these chemicals. No one wants to listen to me, but someone has to." He told me a story about a woman who discovered how diseases were carried in wells in some area (I forget what disease it was), and how housewives are important, and how a housewife discovered this problem and is now famous because of her discovery. All I said was: "Look. This is our problem. I don't care how it was discovered. I don't care how it related to women who discovered diseases in wells. All I know is, this is our problem, and everyone is ignoring it." The senator said that if I needed any help with the studies or if we needed people, he would get them. That lifted our morale some. We began to feel that maybe somebody was finally going to help. But Senator Moynihan did little directly for the residents of Love Canal. He held a Senate hearing, and in 1980 he and Senator Javits tried to get funds for relocation; but we got little assistance from the federal government.

Dr. Paigen was working on the swales data we had collected. We tried to meet with the state health department to compare what we had with what they had; but they refused. I knew some residents hadn't filled out the health department's survey properly, either because they didn't understand or because they didn't want to tell the health department certain things. For example, one person who had epilepsy still had a driver's license. He didn't want to tell the state because he was afraid of losing his license. After a lot of talking and arguing, the health department finally agreed that Dr. Paigen could come to Albany for a meeting to be held in early November. She and I worked hard to make sure all the figures were correct, spending a lot of time on the phone re-checking, to be sure.

On Halloween, I was at the office preparing some things for her. Meanwhile, my children were at home, waiting for me. Six o'clock came, then seven, and I still didn't show up. I finally called my mother and asked her to take them out trick-or-treating, but only on 101st Street. I trusted the people over there. Some families on some of the other streets didn't agree with what I was trying to do, and some didn't like me. I was afraid of what they might give my kids.

Before Love Canal, I never would have missed taking the children out. Halloween, Christmas, Thanksgiving, and birthdays were very important to me and I wanted my children to enjoy them. I wanted to be home in the worst way. It was the same with my other sister's wedding the previous August. Michael was supposed to participate in the wedding, and I had to get his tuxedo. I was late getting home, and I had to help him get dressed very quickly. I wanted to practice walking up the aisle with him, but I just didn't have time.

But I couldn't give up what I was doing. If I did, Michael or Missy might eventually develop some horrible disease. It hasn't been easy on Harry either. Sometimes I told him I wanted to move away. He reminded me that we would leave all our money in this house, and that we couldn't pay for two places. Harry had worked very hard to save the money for the down payment. I can see his side; but, at the same time it tore both of us up—and we aren't the only ones by a long shot.

In early November, Dr. Paigen finally went to Albany to meet with the health department. She had everything prepared, all the statistical correlations and tables. I didn't go to that meeting. When she came back the next day, she was excited. She thought something was going to come of it. Then we read in the newspaper that the state said there was no evidence to back up the swale theory. They said there was no data to back up the claim. All we had was what people told us. It didn't mean anything because it was put together by a bunch of housewives with an interest in the outcome of the study.

Dr. Paigen was furious. She is a careful scientist, and she knew how carefully she had made us collect the information. We didn't count something just because someone said he was nervous. We counted it as a central nervous system problem if the person had actually been hospitalized. People don't tell you things like that for the fun of it. They don't tell you a baby died in the crib just to make up something about an illness for a lawsuit. Beverly was angry because she thought the meeting had gone well. During the meeting in Albany, she said they tried to show that the swales weren't where we said they were. She used clear-plastic overlay maps, with the streets on one, the swales on another, and different color dots for each illness on separate overlays. When the health department officials said the swales were not where we said they were, Beverly asked them to show us where *they* thought the swales were. Well, when they drew their swales in on the map and put on the overlay with the illnesses, it fit even better. So Beverly had good reason to think the meeting went well.

The news reporters wanted to know why I told everyone that the meeting went so well when it had gone badly. It's hard to explain something you don't understand. But we should have expected it. To this day, I haven't learned to anticipate the duplicity of government officials. They say one thing and then do something else. I still haven't accepted that, and, in a way, I hope I never do. I want to think I can trust my government. That's the way I was taught, and that's the way it's supposed to be. It was so sad. Here was proof. Here was evidence. How could they discard it without even investigating? You would think that if they really cared about people's health, they would have said: "Thank you very much for bringing this to our attention. We will look into it carefully." But they didn't. Instead, they put it—and us—down. They attacked the credibility of a damned good scientist, Dr. Paigen, with that crack about housewife data. That is simply wrong.

Carrying on the Fight after the Election

The next phase of Love Canal began after the election and continued until February 8, 1979, when Dr. David Axelrod, the new health commissioner, issued another order allowing pregnant women and families with children under the age of two to be removed from the area. The state checked our data with their own and accepted the swales theory. They offered to move people temporarily. We still had to fight them all the way. Some of the residents became impatient; they wanted to take more radical action. Later, that group almost split up the association.

We asked the state to have a meeting with us in mid-November, to bring us up-to-date on the environmental and health studies. Dr. Haughie, the deputy health commissioner, would hold a meeting for informational purposes; but they didn't seem anxious to answer any of our questions. They wanted us to know what they wanted to tell us and that's all.

In the afternoon before the meeting, Dr. Haughie gave a slide presentation, with maps and data. Although I had a lot of questions, I nearly fell asleep, his presentation was so boring. His monotone voice just went on and on, never rising or falling.

First, Dr. Haughie said there were twenty children with liver problems or who had abnormal liver enzymes, on 100th, 101st, and 102d streets. They were going to do further testing on them. Those streets are all outside the two rings of families that were moved. He said the rest of the liver data came out all right. I didn't understand his reasoning, though, they compared the liver-test results for people living outside rings one and two with those living on rings one and two, and they found no difference. He concluded that everything was all right because the samples were normal for the neighborhood. Well, that seemed plain wrong. Rings one and two were the areas of highest exposure to toxic chemicals. If those areas were in danger, then it seemed to me, so were we. I didn't understand how the health department could reach such a conclusion. At the same time they were trying to tell us the neighborhood was normal, they were also telling us that twenty boys under eight years of age, living two and three streets from the canal, had abnormal liver tests. They were ignoring their own studies.

I told them I didn't think the meeting would go well. I warned them that the residents would get excited if there was no one there who could give them answers, that they would probably be twice as angry at the end as at the beginning. Dr. Haughie kept saying, "Don't worry. It is only an informational meeting."

The meeting began that evening at nine. Dr. Haughie set up the slide presentation. His second slide showed a list of the various chemicals they had found in the Love Canal. The slide was of a computer readout. Some of the lines showed that a chemical had been found; but it was marked Unknown. Someone asked if one of the unknowns could be dioxin. Yes, there could be dioxin in there; but there was a fifty-fifty chance it was not, so no one should worry. By now, the residents were upset. They knew the state had tested for dioxin, and they knew what dioxin would do. They knew it could migrate, and they knew the hazards if you were exposed to it. Someone asked Dr. Haughie if dioxin could migrate; he said no. Because it was not water-soluble, it would not migrate. They also asked him if it could migrate if it mixed with other chemicals like benzene and toluene, which were also in the canal; he said, no. Our consultants had told us that dioxin can migrate with other chemicals. I don't know if Dr. Haughie just didn't know because he wasn't a toxicologist, whether he just got rattled at the meeting, or what.

The state officials don't understand much about communicating with citizens. You can guess what happened. A few days later, there were stories in the newspapers speculating that dioxin had been found. The state said they weren't really sure, or that it was just a rumor. A few weeks later, they announced that there *was* dioxin in the canal. That seemed to be the way it always happened: somebody raised a question or a problem, and the authorities said it couldn't be, that there was nothing to worry about; then, a little while later, it turned out to be true. In the case of dioxin, what they said not to worry about, happened. After this, no one believed the state about anything.

The residents were uneasy. Dr. Haughie didn't get past the second slide because everyone was clamoring to know about the chemicals they had identified in the canal.

About fifty people got up and walked out. They went down the hall to an all-purpose room and held their own meeting. They said they weren't going to put up with the state's baloney any longer; they were going to stop the construction work. People were really afraid that once the state finished the construction project, they would just leave and forget about us. I went back to the meeting. The rest was just as bad. People asked about the health studies, the liver-test findings, the chemicals. But they got nothing but evasions.

Then Dr. Haughie made an unsympathetic, insensitive remark. He said: "We aren't keeping you prisoner here. You people can leave at any time." That was it. The residents couldn't take any more. People just stood up and began yelling at him.

Many residents were upset because the government had just spent $8 million to bring bodies back from Guyana. Those people were already dead and gone; there was nothing anyone could do for them now. But here we sat, being exposed to Lord-knows-what, getting sick and dying. If they could spend money to bring bodies home for burial, they could spend money for people still alive. It was very difficult to understand why the federal government would deliberately ignore us.

Picketing

After another frustrating, emotional meeting we decided to picket the construction work at the canal. The picketing started the following Monday. We made up schedules and decided on our theme. We wanted to emphasize the idea that we were outside the fence, that a chain-link fence couldn't stop chemicals.

The state had put an eight-foot-high chain-link fence around the houses they bought in ring one. The fence was supposed to keep vandals away from the houses and people off the construction site. But the fence made people angry. It became a real symbol. It cost about $58,000, enough to buy two more houses. Meanwhile the fence was a reminder that we were stuck there because of an arbitrary boundary and that the fence could not stop the chemicals from leaking out.

Dr. Jeannette Sherman came to Niagara Falls to consult with Rich Lippes, Dr. Paigen, and me. Dr. Sherman was a physician and a toxicologist. She was surprised, even shocked, by some of the diseases we described, especially some of the bone diseases in young children. She said those diseases were usually found in older people. She kept looking at my notebook, asking if I was sure of what I had written down as the diagnosis. I said: "I never heard of the disease before, and I wouldn't have picked it out of my head." She was awed. I wondered why the health department doctors weren't awed, too.

We started picketing. It was freezing cold at 5:30 that first morning. The lock on my car was frozen. It took an hour and a half to get the engine started. It was eerie when I drove over to the gate on Frontier Avenue. I saw snow-covered, boarded-up houses. There were few tire tracks and footprints in the snow. I looked down 99th Street. It was so peaceful and quiet that I thought for a moment it was a ghost town. It was hard to believe that deadly chemicals were underneath those houses, that poisons were oozing up from under that pure-white snow. It was like a picture postcard of a winter wonderland—if I let myself forget about the boards on the doors and windows of the houses. It was beautiful. Yet the Love Canal chemical time bomb was ticking away, waiting for us, coming at us even if we lived two or three blocks away. *Hooker's* time bomb was ticking away. You couldn't see the chemicals, and you couldn't touch them.

There was a fair-sized crowd at the gate, with newspaper reporters and television cameras. We started picketing early because we wanted to try to keep the workers from going in, or at least to slow them up. We also wanted to inform them about the dangers—to them and us. Everyone was in pretty good spirits. At first we marched around in circles in front of each of the four gates to the construction site on the canal. There was a police car near each gate, with two policemen. When the trucks came, we marched very slowly. Then a policeman would come over and tell us to move out of the way. We tried to tell the workers there was dioxin in there, that they could be hurt, or they could take dioxin home to their families. The workers didn't listen. They went through the picket lines. After awhile, some of the residents chose not to move when the policeman told them to, and they were arrested for obstructing traffic. Chuck Bryan and Marie Pozniak were arrested at the gate where I was marching. They were taken to jail but were later released on their own recognizance. Patti Grenzy who was pregnant got arrested. It was good publicity, if nothing else.

I was arrested the second day of picketing for stopping a school bus bringing bus drivers to go to the bathroom, get a drink, or whatever at the 99th Street School. It was the first time I had been arrested. They had been sitting around in buses all over the neighborhood waiting to evacuate people in case of an emergency. I stood in front of the bus and refused to move, and eventually, I was arrested.

If someone a year earlier had told me I would be arrested for stopping a bus, I would have said that person was out of his mind. I wasn't frightened because I knew from the day before what was going to happen. At the same time, it gave me an eerie feeling to get in the police car with that steel mesh in front of me. The police were very nice. They weren't mean or brutal or vulgar or abusive. They didn't want to arrest us. Many had gone to high school with us. In a way, I was grateful to be in the police car. With the wind chill factor, it was about ten below zero that day, and it was nice and warm inside the car. The TV cameras filmed my arrest.

When we got to the police station, I was frisked just as everyone else was. Then I was put in a cell with a bed. It felt pretty good to lie down and cover myself with a blanket. I had been getting up at five in the morning to make it out to the picket line by five-thirty, and I hadn't been getting too much sleep. When I lay down and looked up at the ceiling, I saw it was made of asbestos. All I could think of was, When is this ever going to end? I come from an environmental disaster, and I'm put in an environmental disaster. There seemed to be no end to it.

My arrest bothered my son, however, even though I was in jail for only a few hours. He wanted to know if I was a bad guy.

Why did I do that? Only bad people got arrested. He was only six then, and couldn't understand. He still asks me about it. I can only hope it hasn't harmed him psychologically.

Picketing continued. I was up early every morning for a week. During that first week, people continued to get arrested. After six weeks, the picketing lagged. People got tired of coming out every morning, and we weren't getting anywhere. We hadn't stopped the construction. All we had accomplished was to aggravate the truck drivers. But it did keep our story in front of the public—and that was important.

The Liver Enzyme Test

While we were picketing, the New York State Health Department notified the physicians of the twenty children whose liver tests were abnormal. The state health department held a meeting with the Niagara County Medical Society to explain what was happening and to ask the doctors to get the children retested.

Without any warning the family pediatrician would call. "We would like your child to come in for a liver enzyme test requested by the state health department." Many mothers had already taken their children for three and four tests. Before, the obvious reason for the test was New York State's incompetence; but when their own pediatricians called, doctors they had trusted for years and years, and those doctors said there was something wrong with their children's blood tests, it aroused all their fears. Parents came into the office crying, wanting to know what was wrong with their children. Why was the pediatrician calling them all of a sudden? Was their child going to die? It was unreal.

I asked the New York State Health Department why they explained everything to the County Medical Society but never said anything to the parents. They could have called the parents individually, to explain they had spoken to the doctors and had asked them to follow up on each child individually. People could have understood if it were explained. But no. All the officials could see was data, statistics, test results.

One parent spoke to one of the doctors, who told her that her child showed signs of toxic hepatitis. That panicked her. She took her child to the local hospital for the blood test. The doctor should have received the results the next day. For some reason, they sent the results directly to Albany. And the poor mother, panic-stricken about her child, had to wait until Albany reviewed the blood test to find out the results.

Some of the residents thought that New York State was fixing the blood tests because they wouldn't allow the physicians to have them first. The secrecy added to the general mistrust of the state among the residents of Love Canal. People felt that nobody cared, that the health department was interested only in its statistics.

Christmas at Love Canal

Christmas came. It was the strangest Christmas I ever had in my life. I can't remember decorating the tree; I can't remember the children opening their gifts. I know I didn't make any cookies. I don't know how the house got decorated, because we were picketing and having association meetings. After picketing, I worked in the office all day. Then I would go to other meetings or to speaking engagements. Many organizations were asking me to speak by now.

So Christmas got lost in the shuffle. That is very sad to me. I remember every Christmas since the day I was born; but this Christmas was lost. I always looked forward to seeing the children's faces when they opened their gifts. I never opened any of my presents until after the kids were done, so I could watch their faces and their excitement. I always loved decorating the tree. I used to hang the tinsel carefully piece by piece. This year I threw it on. We had Christmas dinner, but I hardly remember it. There went a whole year out of my life—Michael's birthday, Missy's birthday, Christmas—three of the most important times of the year were lost to Love Canal.

Fear of the New York State Health Department

The New York State Health Department is very powerful. By law, it exercises a great deal of control over medical facilities, and it spends a lot of money contracting for various services with physicians and scientists. I discovered the extent of this power in a very personal way. Michael had a urinary problem. My doctor told me he might have a bladder obstruction. The diagnosis upset me. Michael had a possible liver problem; he had epilepsy, respiratory problems, and a chronic ear infection—and now this poor child might also have a bladder disorder!

When Michael's convulsions first showed up, I was afraid he had a brain tumor. I called Dr. Axelrod and asked him if urinary infections were caused by chemicals. I knew perfectly well they were. He said, yes, some urinary infections are; but he wanted to wait and find out what Michael had before he was willing to say it was caused by chemicals. I made an appointment for Michael with a urologist.

Since our house was contaminated, I wanted Michael tested to determine what was being excreted through the urine. Those tests cannot be done in an ordinary laboratory. Most of them aren't equipped to do the special testing that's required. Dr. Steve Kim, at the health department, referred me to a man at Cornell who tested race horses and other animals for chemicals in their feed. I asked him if he would be willing to test Michael's urine. I was willing to take Michael there, or to send him a frozen urine sample. He told me he wouldn't do it, that he didn't want to be in conflict with New York State. A scientist in another laboratory he referred me to told me the same thing—that he could do it, but he wouldn't because he didn't want to risk a conflict with the New York State Health Department. The scientist said New York State had the facilities. Why didn't I ask them to do it?

I called Dr. Kim again and asked him why he hadn't told me New York State could do the testing. He said it was because the New York State Health Department's laboratories did testing for Hooker, and there might be a conflict of interest there. That floored me. Talk about a conflict of interest! New York State was suing Hooker! Wasn't it a conflict of interest if the lab did tests for Hooker? Of course, every study the laboratory did would be a conflict of interest; if something were wrong, it would cost the state money. Dr. Kim admitted that he had the people to do it and the laboratory capability; but he wouldn't do the test for Mrs. Gibbs. If he did it for her, he would have to do it for everyone at Love Canal who requested it. Therefore, he wouldn't run the test at all.

Dr. Kim referred me to still another laboratory, this one in Detroit. When I called the lab there, they asked what chemicals were found in my home and in what quantities. I gave them the air readings in micrograms per cubic meter. The person I talked to said the test would have to detect parts per billion or, for some chemicals, parts per trillion, and asked if there were any lawsuits pending. I said yes, and he asked if the results would be used in court. I told him I would be willing to waive the use of the tests in court, but he was very hesitant. Finally he said he would do it—for $2,000.

I called several universities, and each said the same thing. They were capable of doing the testing, but they just didn't want to get involved in a lawsuit with the New York State Health Department. Everyone seemed to be afraid of the health department or a lawsuit—the colleges, the laboratories, the doctors. The professors get grants from New York State; the doctors get their licenses from the state. The veterinarian at Cornell was licensed and received grants or contracts from the state. Nobody wanted to risk a conflict with the health department because of all their power.

To Keep Going

Our problem was to keep going, even though it was difficult, frustrating, and unclear that we would achieve our goals. We also had some real problems within the association. Some of the people who came to help with the picketing, students and some self-styled radicals, tried to dominate it. They said we needed an organizational structure to allow grass-roots participation. I wondered who they thought Marie and Debbie and Grace and I were. They argued forcefully that we should have bylaws and an organizational structure. I thought the association was working pretty well so far without all those pointless rules and regulations. I started several committees because I felt I had to do something to combat what they were doing. They found some residents who were disgruntled and tried to create dissension among the people. The students and others who came over to help with the picketing tried to say that I was the enemy or that Rich Lippes was the enemy.

I still don't understand why they did that, but it was something else I had to deal with. It was bad enough that we had to fight the state, work with the residents, maintain an office, picket every day; we had to resist people who were trying to dominate our organization. Some residents were jealous of others because of publicity one or another received. Sometimes I just wanted to throw my hands up and walk away. It seemed more than I could take; but Debbie, Marie, Grace, Rich Lippes, Steve Lester, and others all helped each other, and we stuck with it. We had to.

People outside Love Canal don't completely understand our problems. I was a guest on many talk shows and other television broadcasts. By this time, I had gotten better at it. I was less frightened than at first. I planned what I would say, and somehow I would manage to get it in no matter what the host wanted me to say. I hoped that if enough people understood, they would write to their congressman in support of us.

Dr. David Axelrod became commissioner of health in January 1979. His appointment made me feel hopeful because he was a scientist. Whalen impressed me as a politician. I thought that if anything would be done, Axelrod would do it. When he became commissioner, I asked all the residents to send telegrams to him as another form of carrying our case forward. I was hoping that with him as commissioner, we might all be relocated. Because of his reputation, I didn't think he would play politics with Love Canal.

In January 1979 I received the results of the air samples taken from the upstairs of my home, showing levels of both benzene and toluene. I again panicked. I thought before that if I kept the children out of the contaminated basement they would be safe. Well, I was wrong. There were chemicals upstairs as well. I didn't know what to do. Michael was going in the hospital to be evaluated for surgery because of his bladder obstruction. Benzene is known to give people cancer and other illnesses, and now there was no way to live in my home and keep my children safe. I had heard the residents talk about having chemicals upstairs; but when it happened to me, I understood their feelings better. I had purposely cleaned my house to make sure the reading was a true one. I removed the cleanser, the soap dish, and the dishwashing detergent. I even took the toothpaste out of the medicine cabinet —everything I could think of. Still, the reading came back positive. The chemicals in the air in my home had to be migrating from Love Canal. Until then, I hardly had time to be frightened. But when this came, and with Michael's surgery coming up, I was really frightened.

Congressman LaFalce was trying to help us by having funds for cleaning up such places as Love Canal put in the "Superfund Bill." When we heard about it, we went to his office with some signs saying we supported him. But he was very leery when he saw us coming. He was in the midst of a press conference. When he saw our signs supporting him, though, he was relieved. If I imagined a year earlier that I would be chasing Congressman LaFalce with signs, well, I wouldn't have, that's all. I am not a sign carrier. Radicals and students carry signs, but not average housewives. Housewives have to care for their children and their homes. But here I was giving press interviews, doing radio programs, and chasing a congressman, a governor, and the President with signs saying I supported him or that he was doing something wrong. Here I was literally screaming at the New York health department or the department of transportation. I never even knew those commissioners existed before all this. Now all of a sudden, I was in the middle of it—and I wasn't really used to it yet. It all seemed strange.

Michael entered the hospital for surgery. He had been out of the Love Canal area only twenty-four hours when, all of a sudden, his stricture was gone according to the diagnostic tests; they didn't need to do the surgery after all. I was angry. The poor kid had to stay in the hospital for three days, all for nothing. I thought maybe the doctors didn't know what they were doing, but when I talked to Bev Paigen, she said maybe his stricture wasn't a stricture; maybe it was an irritation from chemicals filtering through his urine. Maybe the chemicals inflamed his urinary tract so there is a blockage there, but that when he was removed from the area, the blockage ceased. It made me stop and think.

I called Dr. Axelrod for suggestions. He said it might be true, but then it might not. He didn't know. In other words, he wasn't willing to stick his neck out. Within twenty-four hours after I brought Michael home he started wetting himself, and every earlier symptom returned. I did have chemical readings in my home; my house was on a swale. Michael's symptoms disappeared when he was in the hospital; when he returned home, his symptoms returned. I knew I had to get him out of the Love Canal. I just didn't know how or when.

We were still working with the politicians, but nothing seemed to be moving. Everything was so quiet it was frightening—except for the horror stories; they continued. A woman who couldn't sleep called me one night because her dog was going to be put away. It had a liver cancer. She wanted to know if we would take the dog's body to have its tissues studied. I called Albany the next day. No, they did not want any more dogs; no, they would not do the tests. If they had done the test, they might have learned something. It occurred to me that they didn't *want* to find out anything. They didn't want to prove anything.

If we were going to get anything, it would be by doing it ourselves. We held a raffle to raise money. We continued to do interviews on radio and television, and we spoke to many groups. Then we decided to do another health survey. Someone from the New York State Health Department once asked me, half-kiddingly, whether I did surveys just to bug them, or because I had legitimate ideas. I guess it was both. Every time we did a survey, we released it to the press. Then they had to drop everything and run around to find out whether our results were true, just so they could respond to the press.

We decided to do a survey of relocated residents. The results surprised even us. We contacted 101 families and asked them if there had been any changes in their health since they had moved from the area (about six months earlier). Of the homes polled, sixty-seven said a family member's health had improved. They provided us with specific details to show how they had improved. One of the most frequent responses was that people hadn't had any migraine headaches since moving. One woman had a child who was completely deaf. The child hadn't been allowed to take swimming classes because something was wrong with the tubes in her ears. After they moved, her hearing returned to normal. Her mother said it was a miracle. It was remarkable how many people had improved. Not one person surveyed told us they had gotten worse. Thirty said there was no change, and we couldn't tell about four others. They told us of asthmatic children who no longer needed medication, and of people who had ear infections and bronchial infections that just went away or they didn't have nearly as much of it as they had had before. We released the results to the press and mailed the survey to the State. We gave it to the press in order to get a response from the health department. We wondered why they hadn't done the follow-up themselves.

Moving Pregnant Women and Children under Two

Some of our activities were showing results. The health department called a meeting with the residents for February 8, 1979. The meeting was similar to the August 2 meeting, except this time they had health department officials there to answer questions. Everybody knew something was going to happen. Everyone was making guesses, even the media people. Some said there would be no relocation. Others said they were going to move the people in the southern section. Others predicted the relocation of pregnant women and children under two. We made signs. We had fun doing it. It was hectic and it was tense. We were laughing and wondering at the same time.

At the meeting, we all wore blue ribbons because a blue-ribbon panel of experts was supposed to have reviewed everything and made the decision about what to do with us. It was a secret panel, however. No one was identified. We were told they were experts in various health fields, but we didn't know what their expertise was or what their qualifications were. For all we knew, they were the same blue-ribbon panel that had decided whether there would be gambling in Niagara Falls. Bev Paigen's blue ribbon said she was an expert on useless housewives' data. I was an expert on listening to New York State bullshit. Marie was an expert on something else. She wore a blue ribbon with a big question mark. Debbie was an expert on blue-ribbon panels.

Wearing our ribbons, we went into a private meeting with the commissioner. Dr. Axelrod said he had ordered that pregnant women and families with children under two, who lived between 97th and 103d streets and between Colvin and Frontier, should be relocated until the children were two or the area was declared safe. At that time, they could return to their homes. The state was going to pay their moving and relocation expenses and their rent; the residents would keep up the payments on their mortgages. I couldn't believe what I was hearing. If pregnant women and children under two were at risk, so were the rest of us. I knew the way that would go over with the five or six hundred people I was expecting at the auditorium that night.

I badgered Axelrod. I asked him why only those people. Why not women who could conceive? After all, the first fifty-five days are the most important time for damage, and many women don't even know they're pregnant—not for awhile, anyway. I said: "You're telling me the women have to get pregnant and risk the possibility that the fetus will be damaged before they even know they are pregnant, and then they will have to wait several weeks before they can move. That's crazy! You can't play with people's lives!" I asked him if the state was practicing birth control. He said, "No"; but now people could make their own estimates of the risk. Once women knew what risks were involved in getting pregnant at Love Canal, it was their responsibility to decide whether or not to get pregnant. That was another crazy statement. I don't know the risk. It is more of a risk than smoking a pack of cigarettes, or less? Ordinary people aren't qualified to make those judgments. People shouldn't have to make a decision about where they are going to live before they have a baby. I told him he was going to have a hell of a time convincing the residents when he went in to the public meeting.

Reporters and TV cameras from everywhere, including Alaska, were at the public meeting. The national networks were represented. We had signs all over the place—DIOXIN KILLS—things like that. You could feel the tension. The residents were very quiet, waiting for Commissioner Axelrod's statement. He barely got halfway through reading his order before the residents reacted. Of course, the rumor had gone out about what the order was going to say before the meeting began. One of the women in the back of the auditorium got up and screamed: "You can't play games with my life. You have no right to make me stay here. If it is going to hurt pregnant women and children under two, it's going to hurt me." She was crying and shaking, and tears were running down her cheeks. She kept saying, "You have no right to play with my life. You have no right to make me stay here." A man stood up and said: "It's too late for my wife. She's already six months pregnant. What do I do if I have a monster because you wouldn't move us out before?" Residents called out: "The blue ribbon panel—*who are* they? What are they experts in? Where do they get off making a decision about my life?" "You looked at the swale data and decided they were correct as far as birth defects and miscarriages go. Where's the rest of the data?" Some people started blasting the federal government. "This is as much a disaster as a flood or a tornado. We need aid from the federal government, because without it, the state isn't going to move us."

The meeting lasted between four and five hours. The residents were very emotional. Some of the men were crying. Grace McCoulf stood up and said she was planning on having another child, but she did not want to conceive at Love Canal. "You can't make me have a baby here. I want to have a baby, and I'm getting older. I want to have my baby before I am thirty. After that, I take an added risk. You should relocate me and anyone who wants children in the future."

Dr. Axelrod justified everything by saying he was waiting for additional data, that all the data aren't in yet. Just be patient, he asked. We are working as fast as we can.

It's two years later, and the data still aren't all in.

I went home wondering what else we could do. We have

done so much. But we found something else to do. We decided to look at birth defects at Love Canal and block them off in four-year periods. When we did this, we found that nine of the sixteen children born in the last four years, fifty-six percent, had birth defects. We called the state right away and told them what we had found. We asked them to check their records to see if they came up with the same thing. They started off by saying our data were wrong, that we didn't know what we were talking about. They said we hadn't counted all the children in the area. We gave our findings to the press, because that was the only way we moved the state. They were supposed to be checking out all new pregnancies, but if they did, they still haven't said what they found.

I took a survey on my street, 101st, thinking I might get pregnant just to get out of Love Canal for two years. Two children had been born on 101st since February 8, 1978, and both had birth defects. One had six toes and the other, club feet. That alternative was gone. I didn't want to take a chance on having a malformed child just because we had to get out of Love Canal. I couldn't afford to stay, and I couldn't afford to leave. I didn't know whether all of the fighting with the state was going to help. It took us so long to get so few concessions.

Keeping the Media Interested

We had to keep the media's interest. That was the only way we got anything done. They forced New York State to answer questions. They kept Love Canal in the public consciousness. They educated the public about toxic chemical wastes. One day, we decided we'd take a child's coffin and an adult coffin to the state capitol and give it to Governor Carey. It was a way of keeping us in the news. It would demonstrate our plight, and it would give us something to do. We couldn't keep our organization going without some action, some hope.

Lynn Tolli made the baby coffin. She did an excellent job. It looked real, as if a child were in it. We also got an adult coffin, but when Debbie and Harry went to get it, they picked up a real one instead of a cardboard one. They had to take it back and get the other one, especially after the man from the funeral parlor called and said that there was supposed to be a body in that one! We got things straightened out and left for Albany.

We held a press conference at Love Canal at 5:30 the next

morning and then drove to Albany. It was a long drive, and the police kept tabs on us all the way up Route 90. Everywhere you turned, there was a police car. We found the state capitol, parked, and took the coffins out. Mike Nowak carried the coffin over his shoulder up to the capitol. When we got to the front, a police SWAT team checked the caskets. That was really humorous; we parked right behind the police car. When we brought the child's casket to them to check, Marie thought the police procedure was so absurd, she burst out laughing. The news people thought she was crying, so it turned out to our benefit. Did they think we were going to blow up the capitol? Why would we do that? We are law-abiding citizens, not crazies or radicals.

Dr. Jeffrey Sachs, a dentist who was an aide to the governor, accepted the caskets and said he would personally deliver them to the governor, who was in New York City at the time. We stayed awhile to talk with Dr. Sachs and Dr. Haughie, the deputy health commissioner. Both of them tried to tell us about all the health problems in the South Bronx, that Love Canal wasn't the only place with problems. They told us there were health problems all along the New Jersey Turnpike. I lost my patience and said: "Look! I'd like to bring you back to Love Canal, both of you. Love Canal has a definite problem." I described some of them. One of the men complained that they couldn't have any more children because his wife kept having miscarriages. Marie talked about her daughter's asthma.

The Albany media people were there, but they were different from the reporters we had come to know at Love Canal. The media people in Niagara Falls and Buffalo were always sympathetic. In Albany, they kept badgering us. They kept saying, "Well, why don't you just move, Mrs. Gibbs? Why don't you just get up and move?"

Many people ask us the same question. I was fit to be tied. It was all I could do to control myself, and answer one woman. I tried to explain that we lived on $150 a week take-home pay. We had sick children, house payments, and other debts. Our situation was similar to that of our neighbors. People just couldn't pick up and leave. It is very hard for others to understand. If you owe five thousand dollars on a thirty-thousand-dollar house, you would be walking away from twenty-five thousand dollars, perhaps your only savings. Even if you were to do that, you couldn't afford an apartment while you were trying to keep up the house payments, the taxes, the insurance—and hope nobody destroyed the empty house. If you defaulted on the mortgage, your credit would be ruined. I tried to explain it, but she didn't want to hear about it, or try to understand it. They don't live with Love Canal every day.

The next day I had an opportunity I had wanted for a long time. An out-of-town radio station put me on the same program with Bruce Davis, the manager for Hooker in Niagara Falls. Actually, he worked for Occidental Petroleum. He's the man whose picture you might have seen in all those full-page ads that said, "Bruce Cares. And don't let anybody tell you differently." Of course, they stopped running the ad about two weeks later, when Bruce showed how much he cared by transferring to Texas. As far as I know, Bruce, who cared so much, never brought his family up to live in Niagara Falls.

I had wanted an opportunity to confront him, and now I had it. He kept saying Hooker wasn't responsible, that they had warned the board of education. I said: 'Wait a minute. You didn't announce it to the citizens of Niagara Falls. If you had made a public announcement, and the citizens had been aware, there wouldn't have been a school built there, and there wouldn't have been any homes built there." He said, "No, no, no. We had no responsibility. We told everyone about all the problems we knew of. We never had knowledge that chemicals might be migrating out of the canal." He was not telling the full story and I really enjoyed arguing with him. It was something I had wanted to do: have a public confrontation with him. And this time, Bruce Davis squirmed.

At the February 20, 1979, association meeting, Dr. Paigen released a press statement asking the state to relocate 236 families living in the wet areas. The swale theory seemed to be holding up. She said residents who lived on the historically wet areas should be relocated and relocated immediately. She brought a slide presentation with tables and statistical analyses to show to the residents and the press, of which there were many representatives.

She started talking, showing where she thought the wet areas were. First, she showed the slides with the percentages of birth defects, miscarriages, and other illnesses in the neighborhood. Even though I had done a lot of the telephoning with Marie, something about seeing it all up on the screen struck home. I had seen it, and I had talked about it; but something about *seeing* it and *hearing* it made me shudder. All the illnesses and all the statistics up on the screen. It was as if I had been living in a dream world, and all of a sudden reality had hit me. I said to myself: *Lois—this is what you are living with.* Most of the audience sat silently through the presentation. One pregnant woman began to cry and had to go out in the hall. She was so upset, she had false labor pains later that night. The woman was pregnant, but the February 8 relocation order came too late to help her. She was very anxious about the future. How could she be otherwise? The newspapers ran stories about Love Canal illnesses for the next few days.

A couple of months after the slide presentation, in the second week in April, the state reported that they had found dioxin in the canal in concentrations of 176 parts per billion. We decided to hold a rally to protest, mainly because no one else seemed to be paying much attention to this finding. The state released the news on a Friday, probably hoping everyone would be bored with it by Monday. We decided to hold a rally so they *wouldn't* be bored on Monday—or the next Monday, for that matter. We planned to hold the rally at the school parking lot and asked everybody to come. We built dummies of Axelrod and Carey, stuffing them with newspapers and putting old clothes on them. They were great, quite realistic. Debbie Cerrillo, who is a good artist, made the heads. We set the dummies up in the office all day so people could punch them when they felt like it. The rally was at dusk. We started off by walking around the block carrying the dummies, chanting, "Thanks to New York State, Death is Our Fate. We don't want to die—Listen to our cry. We want out!"

Fifty or sixty people came out, even though it was very chilly. Back at the parking lot, I stood up and shouted: "Do you want out?", and they shouted back, "YES!" "Are you going to let the New York State Health Department walk all over you?" and they shouted back, "NO!" It was exhilarating to be in touch with the crowd that way. I had come a long way since that first time, when I was so scared.

It turned out well. We spilled gasoline all over the paper dummies and lit them. It released a lot of frustration to see those dummies burn. The residents were involved; it pulled everyone together. It was a meaningful act to all of us, and we received good media coverage.

Putting a Golf Course on Top of a Chemical Mountain

Niagara Falls had a future-land-use committee. Grace McCoulf and I were on it. The others talked about making Love Canal into a park or a golf course, or a recreation center or a nature trail. It was crazy, and it was ironic. Ten years earlier, when Debbie purchased her home, she was told there would be a park behind her house. Last August, less than a year ago, adults were walking on the canal in halters and shorts, and children were running on it in bare feet. My child played on the jungle gyms and the swing sets. Workers who went on the site during construction wore protective clothing—boots, gloves, and helmets. Some wore gas masks. It was horrible that children were playing barefoot while all the time some government officials knew what was there. Now the future-land-use committee wanted to use the site for a park. Grace and I objected.

You can't put a golf course on top of a chemical mountain. They wanted to put a nature trail in. We don't even have earthworms. We don't have birds. We don't have squirrels. How were they going to put a nature trail in? Nature isn't going to come over to a chemical dump. Animals have better sense than people do. Grace and I had some fierce fights with the mayor and with the committee members.

We thought the canal bed should be covered with grass, but that people should not be allowed on it. It is not safe for people, and no one can convince me otherwise.

We won't know whether the construction and the clay cap are effective. I'm concerned that even if New York State knows the canal is unsafe, state officials won't say so. They spent $30 million or more at Love Canal. Whether it is safe or not, it will be seen as safe—just because the bureaucrats say it's safe. They have too much at stake—their lucrative jobs. It's difficult facing angry citizens and taxpayers.

3

THE
KILLING
GROUND

About the time I was beginning to receive public recognition as a spokesperson on the Love Canal problem, and other Love Canals around the country, I had the greatest trouble within the association.

I now had to spend a great deal of time on association problems. This person didn't like that one. That one couldn't get along with this one. One group didn't like the bylaws. They would have meetings by themselves, and sometimes they would even come over to my house at night to demand this or that. They would criticize what we were doing, and how we were doing it; but you didn't see many at the office offering to help. They kept bringing up the bylaws and saying that I was just putting them off. One person who wasn't even a resident was trying to exploit the situation. He thought he could take over the organization and use it to start a working-class revolution.

I usually go to the office before ten o'clock, but one morning I didn't get in until 10:30. Some of the opposition group started screaming at me because I was late. They didn't "have all day to sit around and wait for me." What was I doing? Why was I coming in late? Was this how I ran an office? It made me angry. Here I was in every single day, working my butt off for these people, and because I was a half-hour late, they carped. I wasn't being paid

and I didn't owe them anything. They had paid a dollar to join
the association, and they wanted their dollar's worth.

National Recognition

I received an invitation to give testimony in Washington before
Congressman Gore's hearings on toxic wastes. Dr. Paigen had
also been invited to testify. I had no idea what to do or how to
give testimony, but it sounded exciting; so I accepted. Steve
Lester worked for a company in Washington and was our consultant. Members of his firm frequently testified before Congress. I
asked him to help me. We worked closely over the weekend. I
am not afraid to ask someone for help when I don't know something, and I'm not afraid to try to find out when I don't know. I
don't see any point in making believe that you know when you
really don't.

I went to Washington with a good friend of mine, Addie
Levine, a sociologist at the University of Buffalo. She was doing
a study of Love Canal. The trip was pleasant and we had a lovely
dinner; but every once in awhile, it seemed unreal. I couldn't be
casual about testifying before Congress. Two congressional aides,
Dave Nelson and Lester Brown, joined us for dinner. A man from
Bloody Run was also there. Bloody Run is a creek in another part
of Niagara Falls. It's called that because it often runs red from
chemicals dumped in it by Hooker. They found that the creek
bottom was covered with dioxin. And people were living near
the creek!

After dinner we went up to my hotel room and went over my
testimony. Later we went to Lester Brown's office. He asked me
to tell him the questions that I would like them to ask Dr. Axelrod,
who would also testify the next day. He wanted to bring out the
issues I thought were important.

I told him what I thought, but I was bothered afterward.
What if I had been on the other side of the fence at this congressional hearing? It was almost as if they were arranging the hearing
to come out the way they wanted it to. What if they had gotten
to someone the night before, to find out what they could ask that
would belittle me? That seemed strange—and shocking. It didn't
seem completely honest, either. I thought I would have my say
and other people who were testifying would have theirs. Then I
thought the congressional committee would weigh the testimony

and reach a conclusion. It didn't work out that way. It seemed as if everything had been decided in advance. I was grateful to be on the right side of the fence at this hearing.

The next morning, after breakfast, we went up to the House. When we entered the building, I had to open up my pocketbook and show that I didn't have a bomb. I wasn't used to that. We went in. The room was packed. We waited for the hearings to begin. We hoped Dr. Paigen would testify before the lunch break, because we expected the media to leave after that.

I was by the bell that called the congressmen to the floor for a vote. A witness would be at a table with a microphone in front of him, with congressmen on either side of him. All of a sudden the bell would ring, and all the congressmen would get up and run out; and there was the poor witness, left talking to the one person still at the table. Eventually the congressmen would come back. I found this procedure strange. How could they hold a hearing when they had to leave every few minutes?

Dr. Paigen was to begin her testimony shortly before lunch. They asked her to cut it short. She was very cool. She glanced at the note someone handed her and said, "Oh, I am sorry I have to cut my statement short so we can go to lunch. We can continue in another room if anyone wishes." She did get through some of her testimony, but the press left before she finished. I had hoped her testimony would be shown on national television.

We went to lunch with Congressman LaFalce. We walked through a tunnel that seemed to go on for miles. Finally we reached the Capitol Building, where we were to have lunch. Congressman LaFalce introduced us to everyone that walked by as his friends from Niagara Falls.

I was supposed to testify that afternoon after Beverly. Commissioner Hennessy kept asking me to follow him. He had to catch a plane. I said no. I wanted to follow Dr. Paigen because our testimony told a complete story. After we got back from lunch, Beverly resumed her testimony. Then they called Hennessy. Addie Levine objected. "Wait a minute," she called from the back of the room. Hennessy turned around and said: "Well, I will be a gentleman and let the ladies go first."

At the end of my testimony, they asked me what questions I would like them to ask Dr. Axelrod when he appeared to testify the next day. I told them to ask him if it would be safe for my children to walk barefoot in the mud in my backyard. I have mud in my backyard because grass won't grow. When I had

finished, Congressman LaFalce said he was going to nominate me
for an award, that if they could give out college degrees, they
would certainly give me one.

We returned to Buffalo, but the day wasn't over yet. We
went straight from the airport to the University of Buffalo for a
forum on Love Canal. I was supposed to speak. That is probably
why Addie Levine was so tough on Hennessey: she was one of the
people who had organized the forum.

Contemplating Pregnancy

While I was in Washington, the Love Canal problems continued.
Near the end of March, Grace McCoulf wrote a letter to her doctor
saying she was contemplating pregnancy. He wrote a letter recommending that she be removed from the area before she conceived.
I called Dr. Haughie and asked him whether her case qualified her
under the February relocation order. The answer was "No."
Now that she knew the risks, she could make an intelligent decision before she became pregnant. I asked him why he thought
that. She wasn't a scientist. He couldn't say what the chances
were of having a malformed baby at Love Canal. How could he
expect an ordinary woman, who had no knowledge of toxic
effects, to evaluate the risk? I kept asking, "What is the actual risk?
What is the danger?" Well, he couldn't say. He said that she could
evaluate the risk. She knew there was a problem.

I was beginning to think nothing could shock me, that
nothing New York State did would bother me. But I was wrong.
I asked Dr. Haughie whether the state was practicing birth control.
"You're telling these women not to have babies because there's a
risk. If you say they can evaluate the risk, then you are admitting
there *is* a risk." He said he didn't know whether there was a risk
or not, that he didn't know the individual family or its history.
Grace was capable of evaluating the risk. He kept repeating that
business about "evaluating." I was so frustrated, I hung up on Dr.
Haughie. I could no longer speak to him. I was afraid I would
lose my temper and that that might hurt our cause. I knew I
would have to talk to him again. So I hung up the phone and told
Gracie she would just have to hold tight until Axelrod arrived.

When Dr. Axelrod got there, I asked him. He said that she
should submit her doctor's statement with a letter, that he would
bring it up with the medical panel. They would let us know the

decision. I didn't hear from him for four months. Grace was still contemplating pregnancy. Mike Cuddy said that, because she was contemplating pregnancy, they were contemplating moving her. Once she became pregnant, they would move her. That made no sense. The first fifty-five days are the most important. The state health department authorities were allowing women to conceive. Some wouldn't even know they were pregnant until it was too late and the fetus was damaged.

About this time, Ralph Nader came to Niagara Falls to give a speech. I was thrilled to think I would be sitting next to him at the head table. We told Ralph Nader about Love Canal. We wanted to win him over to our side. Beverly Paigen sat on one side and I on the other. When she wasn't talking, I was. When I stopped, she started. We didn't have very long, though. He gave me a lot of credit in his speech, which surprised and pleased me.

Niagara Falls—The Killing Ground

ABC put on a documentary called "The Killing Ground." Mayor O'Laughlin was terribly distressed. He said the documentary would give Niagara Falls a bad name by claiming that there were dump sites throughout the city. I was invited to watch the show with the mayor, the city manager, and some other Niagara Falls officials. Unfortunately, I accepted the invitation before I had thought the whole thing through. All three television channels wanted to film me watching it. We should have done it at Gracie's house or some place where other residents would be welcome. But I had already committed myself, so I had to go through with it.

I went to the mayor's office. They had an open bar and some cookies, and some sandwich fixings. I felt like an outsider, as if I didn't belong, as if everyone was waiting for me to react.

The mayor made remarks throughout the show. "Listen to what he's saying. It's *not* all over town. It's not. Listen to what he's saying." Someone else said, "Are they still talking about Niagara Falls?" Then they were talking about Louisana. During the commercial break, someone asked me what I thought. I said it was very good and well worth showing. Of course, they all had different opinions about it. The convention center official said: "I will never get anyone in there now, with this on national news. Who's going to come to Niagara Falls for a convention?" I turned to him and said: "Your convention center is worth what our

houses are worth—right now, zero. Now you know how it feels to
be a victim of Love Canal." The city manager asked me if I was
holding the city for ransom. "I have no intention of holding anyone up for ransom," I said. "All I want to do is get the victims of
Love Canal taken care of in the way they should, to have them
relocated."

During the program, when one of the residents was shown
talking about her son, one of them said: "Is that one of your
expert scientists, Lois?" When Beverly Paigen was on talking
about health effects, the mayor said she was unqualified. He said
she wasn't an M.D. (which was true) but a Ph.D. in cancer research, that she didn't know what she was talking about.

I was being attacked—and hating every minute of it. Jim
Clark was on talking about dioxin. The mayor said he was a ditch
digger. I told him, "Jim Clark may not be an educated man, but he
is very intelligent and he fought the war as a Green Beret. Don't
give me this ditch digger business. He knows what he is talking
about. He has read and educated himself, which is more than I
can say for some people in this room." When Marie Pozniak was
on, he asked me if that was another one of our experts. On and
on it went. They were all obnoxious. I was sorry I had come.

The morning before the show went on, the mayor and I were
on "Buffalo AM," a local television show. In the audience were
many Love Canal residents. The mayor, who was upset, was
sitting next to me. He was trying to pacify me because he was
afraid I would blurt something out on TV. He kept on patting my
hand and saying, "That's not true, Lois, is it? That's not true, is
it?" It was ludicrous. The show's producer was great. He patted
the mayor's hand and said: "It's okay, Mr. Mayor. You'll have
your say next time."

The man who did the interview drove us crazy. He kept saying, "Why don't you move out? If it's so bad, why don't you just
all get up and go? If you worry so much about your health, why
don't you move?" He couldn't get it through his head that we
didn't move out because we couldn't afford to. We went back-
stage after the show. Even the producer was upset. It turned out
all right, however. It was good publicity for the Love Canal
problem.

My life was hectic. Every time I turned around, there was
something else. Michael was sick again, and I had to take him to a
new doctor at Childrens Hospital in Buffalo. I had a TV interview
to do. There was a meeting in Wheatfield. Operation Clean was

having a meeting. Every time I turned around, it seemed as if someone wanted me to go to a meeting somewhere.

The horror stories continued. One woman came in talking about her son. She brought his clothes. They were ripped and torn. She told me his face had been burned at Hooker's 102d Street chemical dump site. His clothes were burned, and many parts of his body were burned. He had been in the hospital, where they had put a tent over him. The woman had pictures of his skin. She said Hooker had given her $10,000 in settlement. She took it because the bank was threatening to foreclose on her house. She thought Hooker had taken advantage of her situation—a $10,000 settlement in return for a son scarred for life. I couldn't stand to look at the pictures. The child had pain written all over his face, and his skin was raw. He looked as though he had been skinned alive. I don't know why she kept his clothes. She wanted to know if there were something we could do. It broke my heart to tell her there was nothing.

Dioxin was found in Debbie Cerrillo's front and back yards, in one part per billion in part of the yard and twenty parts per billion in another. It meant the chemicals had migrated from the canal. Parts per billion might damage a person for life, and under certain circumstances, parts per trillion might be dangerous. Debbie cried when she learned the news. To think, her children had played out there! What were the children's chances of getting some illness later on in life? She was terribly upset. It took her a long time to calm down.

I had planned to go on an Easter egg hunt with my family. I was looking forward to going with the kids, finding some eggs, sitting around eating some chocolate bunnies and not doing much of anything else, except just enjoying each other's company. We went to the Easter egg hunt. I was waiting for the Easter bunny to come riding by on the fire truck, when someone came up and said a group of people were holding a press conference with a dioxin expert. They wanted me there. The children and I had been looking forward to the holiday. I wanted to let the kids know their mom was still there, that Mom cared. I told him I wasn't going. My children came first. They could go ahead with the press conference without me. I was taking my children on an Easter egg hunt.

More Goofs

Things were pretty much the same from February until late spring. The construction at the south end was moving toward completion. It smelled awful after it got warm. On some days people with respiratory problems suffered more than usual, and some people with epilepsy seemed to have more seizures. We had insisted on a good safety plan, and insisted they dig outside the canal's perimeters; they did dig carefully and nothing disastrous happened. The state did not keep all its safety agreements and we had to be after them all the time. Once a tank truck filled with leachate leaked, and we had to tell them about it. Even after we showed it to them, they said no, it couldn't be happening. Finally, when they saw it with their own eyes they believed it.

They were supposed to wash down the trucks that were in contact with contaminated ground before the trucks left the immediate vicinity of the canal, but they often didn't do that. We had to keep after them constantly. We were worried they would be tracking dioxin all over the neighborhood. Later that spring, many hedges looked as though they had been defoliated. I was pretty sure it was dioxin from the trucks that had harmed them. The state said· no, that the bushes died of winter frost. *Winter frost!* Those bushes had survived the blizzard of '77. Now some of them looked as if someone had taken a paint brush and painted the tops brown in a slanted line. Bushes just don't die like that. I wasn't worried about the hedges, however. I was worried that whatever had defoliated them was in the air and that we were breathing it.

The state did another one of its real careful, sensitive jobs. They had promised us tax relief. The bill they put through was written in such a way that it drew a line down the middle of 93d Street. The people on one side of the line received tax relief while their neighbors on the other side didn't. Unfortunately, those people didn't blame the state; they blamed *me* for not fighting hard enough for them. After awhile the state changed the boundary line to include them, but first it caused another small citizens group to form and that affected our organization.

The State Bureaucracy

The first meeting we had with the state after the February 8 order

After dioxin was found, the state ordered all vehicles to be washed before leaving the construction area. *Courtesy Stephen Lester*

to temporarily relocate pregnant women and families with children under two, was about the construction plan and the safety plan for the next phase of the remedial construction. The meeting was fairly well attended, but a lot of the people didn't come to talk about safety in construction. It turned into another emotion packed screaming match of homeowners versus New York State. The state people had the meeting all planned. Each one was to give a fifteen-minute presentation, and leave fifteen minutes for a question and answer period. Each person would have to stand up, identify himself and then ask a question. It seemed impossible for them to hold an orderly meeting and be out of there and on their way home by nine o'clock. The residents had many questions; they wouldn't tolerate the state's attempt to control the meeting.

They began the meeting with slides showing the canal's perimeter and where the construction was going to be. After the first presentation, I raised my hand to ask the first question. The man who was running the meeting asked me to identify myself. That put the audience in hysterics. Somebody said: "Everybody knows her. What the hell does she have to identify herself for?" Well, I asked questions, and so did a lot of other residents, especially Art Tracy who is an effective natural speaker.

Art stood up and described his problems—his cellar and his yard—and the levels of the chemical readings in his house. He asked what the state was going to do for him. The man on the stage got up and said, "I'm sorry. I can't answer that. You'll have to ask the health department, and no one from the health department is here tonight. If you will submit your question in writing, I will see if I can get you an answer."

One just doesn't say that to a man who is emotionally upset and trying to save his family. Besides, the state rarely *answers* in writing. You can't tell someone to submit something in writing so he can get an answer. He won't accept that, and neither will anyone else.

The state people wondered why we mistrusted them, why we don't believe what they say. Frank Rovers, the engineer who drew up the construction plan, said that the drainage ditches couldn't get clogged up, that the filters would never get plugged. Well, people who work in factories and in construction know better. They have seen more than one smart engineer with perfect plans take them back to the drawing board. When they heard the state representative say the swales were contaminated by fill that had been dumped from the canal into the swales, some of the residents had a fit. Art Tracy stood up and said that wasn't true. He was an old-timer. He had filled in his own land, and none of the fill came from the canal. When they said they weren't going to do anything outside the canal's perimeter, everybody was upset because their homes were sitting in lindane, chloroform, and many other dangerous chemicals. The meeting turned into a nightmare.

One of the newspaper reporters from the Niagara Falls *Gazette* was there. He asked why the people were talking about health problems when no one was there who could answer any of their questions. I was angered by his failure to grasp the situation. I told him the people were screaming for help. They were hoping someone, somewhere would hear them and help them and their families. They just want to be relocated. Perhaps a newspaper story would reach someone with a conscience who would help them. It made me stop and think: *If this news reporter doesn't understand, and he lives in the area, what does the rest of the world think?*

Eyeball to Eyeball

The next day, Governor Carey came to Niagara Falls. He came to talk to a Convention of the New York State Teachers Union. The governor agreed to meet with us before he went to the Convention Center. They said we could bring three people but not Dr. Paigen. I insisted that Dr. Paigen come, so the governor said that David Axelrod, the health commissioner, would be there. I sent some residents, including my husband and two children, to the airport to meet Governor Carey. He arrived in a pouring rain. He got into his car and started to drive past all the protesting people, when somebody screamed out, "You are a murderer! You are killing my children!" When he heard that, he stopped the car to get out and talk to the people.

Governor Carey seemed annoyed. He told the crowd he was all they had going for them. If they wanted to be so public about it, he would be glad to take their names and make their health problems public knowledge. The residents told him their health problems were already public. They just wanted to be relocated. The governor seemed perturbed and got back into his car. He said he was going to tour Love Canal. According to the residents, he whisked through the canal and then went over to the Hilton Hotel.

Beverly Paigen, Debbie Cerrillo, Jean Hasley and I were at the Hilton. We brought Jean because she could take shorthand. The first to arrive were Commissioner Hennessy, Tom Frey, the governor's aide, and Commissioner Axelrod. Tom Frey asked some questions, and I couldn't resist giving him some smart answers. I don't really know why I did it except that it annoyed Axelrod. Tom Frey asked how I was, and I said I was chemically treated. He asked me if I was pregnant yet. I told him, with a one-hundred-percent birth-defect rate on my street, I wasn't about to get pregnant. Then Axelrod told him to stop asking me normal social questions because I would just answer him with a wisecrack. I asked Axelrod why nothing was being done about the swales—no cleanup and no construction to stop the leaching. "How can you leave people in contaminated areas?" He said they were already investigating it. I said, "You have established that it is contaminated. What are you going to do about it?" He had no answer.

At this moment, Governor Carey came in with the rest of his entourage. Mike Cuddy was with him, as were Paul Wells, his PR man Marvin Nailor, and I-can't-remember-who-else. The room was big, with a U-shaped table. We rearranged the tables into a large square so we could sit around it and see each other.

Governor Carey asked me what I would like to discuss. I was annoyed. I thought it was perfectly clear what I wanted to discuss. I said: "Relocation—for many reasons." I told him that health problems were showing up beyond rings one and two, in the evacuation zone. The New York State Health Department had admitted the danger to fetuses in the areas that were historically wet. Dioxin had been found in very high concentrations in both the front yards and the backyards of the homes on 97th Street, which meant that the chemical was migrating. I told him of the child north of Colvin who had a common childhood disease, normally curable, but who had died from unexplained complications. I told him my child had some of the same symptoms and that I didn't want him to end up the same way as that boy north of Colvin.

Governor Carey just looked at me. I had a news clipping of Luella Kenny's story telling of the family's ordeal and how the child died. I placed it in front of him, forcefully. Dr. Paigen was talking with Axelrod, but I watched Governor Carey. He kept looking at the clipping, reading it, then pushing it away. Then he would read it again and push it away again. I don't know much of an impact it had on him, but he must have skimmed it four times.

Beverly got into an argument with David Axelrod when she tried to talk about the health effects. He belittled her scientific ability and qualifications and said her cancer study was no good. She said she had never done one. What was he talking about? He insisted that she had. Dr. Paigen had never done a cancer study or made any claims about an excess of cancers at Love Canal. In the news release accompanying his February 8 order, he said there was no evidence of other illnesses. She asked him for the evidence backing up his statements, especially since he had made the statements in a news release. They talked for about fifteen minutes. At first, Axelrod didn't seem to want to give her anything at all. Finally, he said he would give her all the past statistics and future ones as well. It is now two years later and the health department still hasn't released studies backing their claims.

After they had argued awhile, Governor Carey asked to look at her data. She handed him her papers so he could see the tables she had prepared. He skimmed them and asked her if she had any medical or laboratory confirmation for her survey findings. She said no, that was a problem in her studies. In that case, he said, they were worthless. As he tossed her papers across the table at her, the papers scattered all over. You could see Beverly's eyes light up. She was mad but she maintained a cool, determined, professional attitude. She stood up, walked around her chair, bent down, and picked up the papers slowly. She sat down again, neatly stacked the papers together in order, and then passed the study back across the table to him. She went on in a very calm voice to explain that she did some of the interviewing and we did some interviewing. She granted that people might overreport illnesses to us, but she pointed out that would be true for people living in the dry areas as well as in the wet areas so that bias was eliminated. They went back and forth. Beverly never raised her voice and was never rude. She just explained the problem slowly and carefully.

At one point she started talking about the anonymous blue ribbon panel. They explained why they wanted to do it that way, but she answered that New York State appeared secretive. That seemed to make Governor Carey defensive. "My health department is one of the best," he said. "We do not have secrets in the New York State Health Department!" Beverly said, "Yes, you do have secrets, Governor Carey, because they will not give us any data. They are hiding it and that makes it secret." He said they did not have secrets. They went back and forth five or six times almost repeating the same words. It looked as if they were going

The school playground, which was found to be contaminated with dangerous chemicals, was fenced off.
Courtesy Stephen Lester

to argue until one of them got tired. I don't know whether Axelrod changed the subject or someone else did.

Governor Carey said that David Axelrod was going to review the residents' records again for temporary relocation during construction just as Governor Carey had promised the residents who met him at the airport. I asked what the criteria for relocation would be. The last time they reviewed on the basis of whether or not the canal was going to blow up. Governor Carey had given us a safety plan that I thought was good. But I told him we wanted to be evaluated because we were living with dangerous chemicals in our homes. David Axelrod agreed residents would be evaluated individually, and to make sure there is no secrecy, Beverly would participate to make sure the criteria are followed.

I continued to insist that all residents from 93d to 103d streets be evacuated. I told him that any woman who was contemplating pregnancy should be removed from the area, because a woman would have to think about abortion in a way she never had to before. He said I was asking to evacuate the whole area, and I said that was right. He said it wasn't possible. Then I went back to talking about my family's illnesses and problems. He told me that he had fourteen children, two dead. I said I was sorry that two of his children were dead, but that if you added up all the illnesses for all fourteen of your children, you wouldn't come up with half the problems my one child has. He repeated, two of his children were dead, and I said, I didn't want any of mine to die. He assured me that wouldn't happen, and I told him I wasn't as sure as he was.

We fought and argued for quite awhile. I lost all of my shyness. I said this is the way it is, and this is what has to be done. He came back and told me he didn't have unlimited resources, that he cannot assure everyone in the state they would have no environmental risks, but he did say he would consider relocating the people.

The first time I met Governor Carey, I felt intimidated, really afraid. Anything he said was fine with me. The second time, I was cautious, but a little more demanding. The third time I was less cautious and more demanding. But the way I talked to the governor didn't hit me until I got home. I talked to him as if he were an average person, not the governor of New York State. I wasn't rude, and I wasn't vulgar, but I was very determined and very angry.

It was difficult dealing with Governor Carey because every

other time I had met him with reporters and TV cameras present. When he answered questions, he had to make sure the answers came out to his advantage, and that he came out looking OK. This time we met behind closed doors, and it was a different Governor Carey. He sat there stonewalling. Anyway, I never believed that I could have talked to Governor Carey that way. I spoke right up and I was very firm. Beverly Paigen, though, was fantastic. I never saw anyone so determined and so brave. Because Beverly works at Roswell Park, Health Commissioner Axelrod is her boss, indirectly, and of course she is a state employee.

Later, the governor went across the street to Convention Hall to address the Teachers Union. We had about seventy picketers out there. The prison guards were on strike at that time, and they also had protestors and picketers out. I talked with some guards from Attica, and we all joined together in protesting and chanting. Governor Carey spoke at the beginning of the convention; then he left. I regretted that he wasn't there when they passed a resolution in support of us. I went up to the balcony of the auditorium with Murray Levine, who has a little mischief in him. I wanted to put a sign out over the balcony, but I didn't because I was afraid it would hurt my credibility after I had had the private meeting with the governor. I left and Murray hung up the sign. All in all, it was helpful to our cause.

Pull Together or . . .

We had a task-force meeting in May. We presented our list of demands. The meeting took place in the school's gymnasium. Commissioner Hennessy, New York Department of Environmental Conservation Commissioner Flacke, and Health Commissioner Axelrod were there. Hennessy and Axelrod took turns leaving the meeting and returning. Commissioner Axelrod has a conscience, unusual for a politician. Axelrod didn't seem to be able to look me in the eyes. When I asked him a question, it seemed as if he couldn't look at me. He put his hands on the table and looked at his fingers, or he looked to the right of him or in front of him, anywhere but where I was sitting. It was the expression on his face. I felt as if he knew that what he was saying wasn't right, and he couldn't really admit it in the open.

Some residents formed their own organization to fight for their taxes. The state had promised us some relief from our property taxes because they agreed our houses were worthless on the market, but the bill they put in the state legislature set the boundary on a line down the middle of 93d Street. The residents on the other side were pretty upset, and some formed their own organization to fight for their taxes. They had a representative at the task-force meeting. The woman who came reminded me of myself because she was so intimidated by Commissioner Hennessy. We asked him what he was doing about the taxes, and Hennessy turned to her to answer the question. He said he didn't know what was going to happen, that it was up to the state legislature, and we will see where it goes from there. She just said, "OK, sir." I thought that was funny; that's how I had acted less than a year ago.

Earlier that day, I received a call from radio station WHLD. They told me I had won the Top Hat Award as Outstanding Citizen of the Month. I was excited, but I couldn't enjoy it. When some of the other residents heard about things like that, they got upset and some said I was in it just for the publicity. Not everybody said it, but enough did.

Right after WHLD hung up, Congressman LaFalce called to tell me he would like to nominate me for the list of Ten Outstanding Young Women of America. Two commendations in one day were flattering, and I was excited about both of them; but I was afraid of what the residents would say when it got into the press. I was afraid some of them would hold it against me. I was sad. The awards were something I should have been able to enjoy instead of having to defend myself because of them.

The day before the task-force meeting, Dr. Vianna had released a statement from the health department saying that no abnormal miscarriage rate, or birth defects, or low birth weights were found at the north end of the canal, north of Colvin. I asked Dr. Axelrod for the data which he and Governor Carey promised a month ago. He said he didn't know what had been released to the press and that it wasn't official yet. When it comes through, I will be glad to give you the reports; same old story. We asked about the relocation review they had promised. He said they were beginning with the fifty-four residents who had submitted their records and who had been rejected back in October when they decided the canal wasn't going to blow up.

The association's meeting in May was important. I learned that people sometimes take out their frustrations on their leaders. By now the people at Love Canal were stretched past their emotional limits. People came into this meeting ready to hang somebody, Debbie, me, anybody, just to hang somebody. They couldn't do anything to the state but yell and scream. The city ignored us. The mayor wasn't even willing to admit there was a problem at Love Canal. At this meeting they thrashed out at the nearest person—me. What else could they do? They were frustrated and fearful they would be left to die, or if they moved they have to give up everything for which they had worked so hard. Some people came to association meetings to vent their anger and express their fears. Sometimes people have legitimate complaints or want me to do something different. But when they attacked me, I came to believe they were really attacking the state for not acting soon enough, for not helping them to relocate, for not saving their babies.

One group wanted Debbie Cerrillo's resignation. She wasn't at the meeting, but she had sent a very moving letter of resignation. I read it very slowly and paused to let it sink into their heads. Then Mrs. Green asked if we accepted the resignation. I said, "No. It will be up to you to decide whether you want Debbie to leave or stay." Lee Lutz, who is a strong speaker, said some complimentary things. We had a vote, and they voted not to accept her resignation.

I had heard rumors that some were going to ask for my resignation as well. I opened the topic first. I said I would be more than happy to resign. If they thought I was in it for the publicity, they were wrong—very, very wrong. Michael was going to the hospital to be evaluated for surgery on Monday. He is a sick little fellow, and I was doing all I could to get out. I was trying to take care of my family. I didn't seek personal publicity. All I wanted was a safe place to live. I wanted out just as everyone else. Somehow it worked. It turned them around.

The Love Canal Homeowners Association was similar to most community groups. We had a small crew who did all the work. Everyone else sat back and let others take care of it for them. Still others just criticized. Many people don't want to be bothered. They have their bowling night, their this, their that. As the leader I had to absorb their frustrations and hope that everyone would stick together in a real crisis.

Hearings and More Hearings: Is Anyone Listening?

The day after one of the task-force meetings, the state senate held a hearing in Niagara Falls. Hooker always testified first, then the State of New York, then citizens, citizen groups, and environmental groups. It happened in the congressional hearings in Washington, in the senate hearing, and in every other hearing I attended. I think they should wait until the citizens get through so the Hooker officials could listen to the people's views.

Mike Cuddy testified for the state. One of the senators asked him how long it would take the state to evaluate the swales to convince them that it was or was not a health problem. Mike estimated two to two-and-a-half years. That upset some of the senators. They asked him if he really expected residents to live there for two or two-and-a-half years and wait to learn if there was a problem. He said he could not answer that. That was the health department's decision, not his. They also asked him why the state hadn't relocated more families. He could not answer. It was the health department's decision.

Then I testified. I spoke about New York State's conflict of interest in conducting studies when certain outcomes could cost them money. I described the lacks in their studies and I emphasized their insensitivity to the people. Marie Pozniak, Laurie Nowak, Debbie Cerrillo, and Nancy Rebon also testified. The hearings started first thing in the morning. They testified late in the day. They went last, but they were great. Of course, Hooker didn't have to wait around all day to be called. Marie and Nancy were in tears when they testified. I think the senators were very moved by their statements and rightly so.

Senator Moynihan held additional hearings in Niagara Falls at the end of May. Beverly and I both testified, but no other residents were called. The first one to testify, of course, was Hooker's Bruce Davis. Hooker said they were good corporate citizens, that they are cleaning up their dumps. They went on to talk about their future plans. I found it nauseating.

Beverly and I had over an hour. We criticized Commissioner Axelrod for not authorizing women who wanted to become pregnant to leave the area. We showed our overlay maps showing the illnesses clustered on the swales and gave the health statistics. Congressman LaFalce also made an excellent statement. He said that if he had a wife in this area, he would never have any children because of the risk involved. That was very helpful. Grace Heubner, Grace McCoulf, Laurie Nowak, Luella Kenny, Joanna Hale, and a few others submitted written statements.

At the end, Senator Moynihan said he would like to hear from a few Niagara Falls residents. Grace McCoulf stood up and gave him the letter she had written to the health department saying she was contemplating pregnancy and wanted to be relocated. The state had not yet acted on it. She said she didn't want to wait until she was much older to have her baby. She wanted to conceive before she took on an added risk of age.

Early in the hearing, Senator Moynihan asked me how I was doing, and when was it he had last seen me. I told him the exact date in October, when he was up, and I said: "As a matter of fact, you made a lot of promises that I plan on taking you up on." Nothing happened at this time, but later after the news that some residents had chromosome breakage, both he and Senator Javits gave us strong support in getting the federal commitment to relocate everyone.

Nothing the State Says Would Surprise Me

At the end of May 1979, we were still working with the people and with the state to set up the relocation review Governor Carey and Commissioner Axelrod had promised us when we met with them. I never thought anything I heard from the state would surprise me again, but I was wrong. I called Dr. Vianna to ask about the progress of the studies. He told me some of the records were missing. I asked about Marie Pozniak's doctor's statement. No, it was missing. I asked about Mrs. Smith's son's record, and for her record. Somehow, these were missing. The records for Mrs. Jones's daughters were missing, and one had a birth defect. I asked Dr. Vianna what had happened to the records. He said he couldn't be responsible for everything that came into the health department.

Because the documents were misplaced we had to go back to all the doctors, and residents, get new consent forms signed, and have all the records resubmitted. Everything had to be recopied. I did it because he assured me, that they were going to do a careful case-by-case health review very soon. The women in the office made sure that all the residents who submitted records for review called the health department to determine which records they had. Each resident asked Dr. Vianna what was missing. Most people cooperated, and as a result we found there were more missing records than we suspected. That upset us. It was like pulling teeth to get the records from the doctors in the first place, or to get them to write letters saying the child or the family should be moved. The Niagara County Medical Society wasn't cooperative at first. To get the records the first time was bad enough, but to go back a second time was impossible. I called Axelrod and complained. He said he would check with Vianna and call me back. I am still waiting for his call. Eventually the missing records were found. We were put to needless effort.

Everytime we turned around, it seemed there was something else to protest. The state decided they would auction off the ring one homes and garages. The people who bought them were to move them by a certain date and fill in the basements. The health department wouldn't say the houses were unsafe, but they refused to say they were safe. They sold only eight homes and eleven garages, I believe. The sale of those homes and garages for three or four thousand dollars didn't help the New York State taxpayer much. One man bought six homes. He planned on moving them out of the area and then selling them or renting them to poor innocent families who wouldn't know they might conceal toxic chemicals or that they were from Love Canal. There was no good reason for the state to sell the houses. The state wouldn't recover much money, and they were running the risk of future litigation.

Our mayor was in favor of the idea of moving the houses, but the town councils of Wheatfield, Niagara, and Lewiston passed resolutions saying they would not issue building permits for those homes.

Back in January, when we were picketing, Hennessy announced that the state had given United Way $200,000 to pay residents' excess medical bills. The contract with United Way made provision for some day-care centers and to send some of the children to day camp to get them out of the area during the construction period, and thus limit the children's exposure. We arranged for a day-care program at the Y. It was a good facility. They had planned activities, a swimming pool.

A few days later I found out that Joe Maloney of the United Way canceled all the plans. Joe wanted the day-care center at the 95th Street School. I couldn't believe he did it after all the work we put in to make the plans and identify the children. The 95th Street School doesn't have any of the facilities the Y has and no planned activities.

I told him parents would not take their kids there. They finally agreed to what we wanted, and we signed up forty-five young children for day care, and a great many older children for the day camp. Maloney had to take money out of another part of the budget to cover all the children. It wasn't too hard to find

Deaf Child Area—a sign in the Love Canal neighborhood indicates one of many kinds of birth defects resulting from contamination. *Courtesy* Niagara Gazette, *photo by John Kudla*

the money in the budget because they set up the rules in such a way that it was difficult to get money for medical expenses anyway. I don't think they spent more than a couple of thousand of the $200,000 on residents' medical costs. Fourteen percent went to the United Way for overhead. More went to pay for secretaries and some United Way salaries. They paid for a conference for mental health workers and to train people who were supposed to go around and give us information. It seemed to me all they did was to hire people who handed out printed pamphlets that told what United Way did. They didn't even try to hire the Love Canal residents who could have used the money and who would have done something for the people. As I said, I thought I was past being surprised, but every day brought its own new one.

How Many More Children Must We Lose Before a Decision Is Made?

It took me a long time to give up the idea that the state and the health department would do what was right and just. Maybe I didn't want to face reality, or maybe it is because I still had some ideals left and believed human beings lurked under bureaucrats. I always believed that if I could just talk to the right person and explain the situation, something would be done. I was disappointed time and time again, but never so much as when a close friend miscarried and lost her baby.

In February, the state finally agreed that our swale theory was right. Commissioner Axelrod issued an order saying that pregnant women and families with children under the age of two could be temporarily relocated. When the idea of moving women who were contemplating pregnancy first came up, we were told a decision would be made in the near future, possibly in two weeks, which would have brought it into the middle or the end of March 1979. The women who were contemplating pregnancy went to their doctors requesting letters stating they were contemplating pregnancy, and that their doctors recommended they be relocated prior to conception. A number of women obtained them and then we began to go through the time-consuming, useless bureaucratic chain.

First, the women submitted their statements to the New York State Health Department. Then they waited. A month went by and no decision. I called Axelrod and asked when we could expect a decision. He said we could expect a decision in two weeks. They (whoever *they* were; they never told us) were going to have a meeting. Another two weeks went by and no decision. Again, I called to ask David Axelrod when we would expect a decision. "In a few weeks. You must be patient," he said. I followed this telephone call with a memo. A few more weeks went by, and there was still no decision. When I met Dr. Axelrod at a meeting in Niagara Falls, I asked again. He said he had made his recommendation to the task force and it was now out of his hands. The task-force members were all political figures. They were not scientists, or physicians. How could they make medical decisions about women in Love Canal? There aren't even any women on the task force.

What was Commissioner Axelrod's recommendation? He wouldn't tell me. Why was everything so secretive? Axelrod said he believed the politicians would honor his recommendation. But if that were true, why was he hiding it? If he believed the women should be relocated, and if he as health commissioner and a physician issued that kind of order or even a statement, the politicians couldn't say no. They keep everything secret and delayed. Nothing gets done, and everyone avoids responsibility for the decision. The first doctor's letter, recommending relocation for a woman contemplating pregnancy, was sent to the New York State Health Department in March. The decision had not been made by the end of July.

During that time, a close friend and neighbor became pregnant. She had submitted her physician's letter in April. She desperately wanted another child. This woman had lived in the Love Canal area all of her life. She had a history of miscarriages, and her only child had a birth defect. She didn't get an answer to her doctor's request that she be relocated before she conceived, and even after her doctor certified that she was pregnant, she still had to fight with the state. They had a regulation about who could be moved after they were pregnant, and what you had to do to prove it and other nonsense. Finally, they decided to put her and her son up in a motel. The motel owner said she couldn't have her dog with her, and when she asked the state to help her, they asked her what was more important, her dog or her health.

She didn't have much to do in the motel room. She used to keep busy cooking, taking care of her house and yard, and working at her hobbies. All she had in the motel room was the TV or silence. She felt useless. With all the time on her hands, she thought a lot about her unborn child, mostly happy thoughts—what to name the baby; what she needed to buy; whom the baby would look like. She was hoping that this time she would carry the baby full term and not miscarry, as she had in her last pregnancy. Then she noticed some bleeding. As time went on, the bleeding became heavier. Eventually, she miscarried.

Because she was a close friend, and because of their delays in deciding to move her before she conceived, I was very upset and very angry. I called the health department and told them I held them personally responsible for the death of that baby. Because they didn't want to set a precedent, or spend the money, or for whatever reason, a human child was sacrificed needlessly. I asked them how many more children we would have to lose before someone would make a decision. There was silence at the other end of the phone. No response. But no response is the answer we always seemed to get.

4

THE
MOTEL PEOPLE

It was now August 1979. Although it had been more than a year, we hadn't given up. Construction began at the north end of the canal. It was different than when they worked on the southern section, because of the heat of the summer. All the things we worried about earlier now showed up. Residents were becoming ill. After the heavy construction on the north end began, the air was humid, hot, and stagnant, and it reeked of chemicals. Over 50 percent of the children were absent from the day-care centers and the camps because of illness. One adult who hadn't had an asthma attack since he was a child, all of a sudden had one and was taken to the hospital twice during one week.

We kept a daily log. Ninety-seven families had called their physicians, seeking medical attention. A few went to the emergency room, and two children were hospitalized. I can't tell you what it was like on some days. It was hot, and the air would just hang there. The fumes were thick. They made your eyes water, or you coughed. Someone described it as similar to trying to breathe underwater. In the winter the cold wind would come off the river and blow the fumes away. That was bad enough, but in the summer, you knew you were living on a chemical dump.

I called Axelrod because I was frightened myself. Both my children were sick, and Missy is usually never sick. Michael had a couple of seizures and was running a temperature. His eyes and ears were irritated. One of our office workers was taken to the hospital because she was having difficulty breathing.

Axelrod told me he would investigate. If I would send him what I had, he would see what he could do.

I went across the street to the state task-force office and tele-copied a list of ninety-four families' names, addresses, their physicians names, whether they saw their physician, or whether they just contacted him by phone, their symptoms, and their diagnoses when they had seen a physician. When I called him the next day, he said he had talked to four physicians. They said that it was something going around and that I shouldn't be concerned. I was really upset with that. The health department had had contact with many of the physicians in Niagara County. They knew which ones would be sympathetic and which ones wouldn't. He may have contacted four physicians, and those four physicians probably said that to him, but he knew the four to contact who would come out and say what he wanted to hear. So, Axelrod said there was no problem, that it was something going around and not to worry about it.

A few residents were temporarily evacuated. When we went to court to try to stop the construction, the judge accepted the state's safety plan. Those who felt ill or who felt discomfort could leave the area for forty-eight hours. A few of the residents decided to go because they were frightened. They didn't want their families to stay in the area during the construction. They were evacuated to Niagara University, a college near Bloody Run. The people didn't know how long they could stay out, but they knew they did not want to come back to Love Canal. They knew that they were sick and blamed it directly on the construction.

The residents were now more anxious than ever—and far more upset. Families were sick, but no one would acknowledge a problem. We decided to do something in the form of protest in order to bring everyone together and get the media back again. That was the only thing that had helped us. We planned a candle-light ceremony to celebrate the first anniversary. We asked the Ecumenical Task Force on Love Canal to arrange for a minister to conduct the service. They refused. No one wanted to be involved. Debbie Cerrillo called the head of her church, who agreed. We held it in the evening at dusk. Many of the media people covered it. The weather was slightly foggy, with a misty rain. It fit everyone's mood. The service left us with a feeling of closeness. Although I am not very religious, the idea that we were all together, whether praying to God or just knowing someone else cared, set the whole mood.

Unfortunately, the following week we needed more than prayers. The New York State Health Department issued a press release stating that they had found dioxin in the leachate collected in the drainage system.

Once again, there was panic. "What should we do? Where did we go?" "Who could we talk to?" There was no one. The state did not have any health department personnel, nor anyone from their laboratories. They did what they usually did: released the news on a Friday in hopes that the residents would calm down by Monday.

A state task force meeting was set for August 21. David Axelrod would be there. The task force meeting was to be closed to the residents. Only task force members were supposed to attend. I told the residents they had as much right to be there as anyone else, that I couldn't ask every question they might have. We preferred a public meeting, but the task-force refused. I explained why the meeting should be open. I told the residents to go to the task-force meeting, stand outside, bang on the door, force their way in. I told them not to be put off because they weren't wanted there. If they made enough noise, they would be let in. The meeting was held in a big gymnasium in the housing project just west of the Canal. The room was so large that every time anyone talked, it echoed. The residents banged on the doors and eventually were allowed in. They sat in front of the U-shaped table but they just couldn't hear anything that was going on. They were too far away; when somebody spoke up, it echoed. Hennessy told the residents to move closer to the table. The residents were inches away from the commissioners, which made them nervous and made me happy. I took a dead branch from across the street. Vegetation was dying in the neighborhood, but no one seemed to care; no one seemed to want to check it. I was going to make sure he saw it, and that he touched it. I put the stick in a plastic bag and I set it underneath my seat, waiting for the right time.

The meeting began and Commissioner Hennessy opened the meeting. He said a few things about nothing in particular. Then I began to go down my list of questions. I had a long discussion with Axelrod about the health studies and their inadequacies. I kept badgering him about the miscarriages and the women who were contemplating pregnancy. I told him about my neighbor's miscarriage. I believed that if she had been out of the area prior to conceiving, her baby might have survived. Axelrod answered with the stupid statement that she had weighed the risks, that she was an intelligent young lady. She knew the risk. I got angry and said: "We *don't know* what the risk is. *You* tell *me* what the risk is. If I were to get pregnant, what would be my chance of having a miscarriage?" He said I knew there had been miscarriages. Finally, he gave in and said the miscarriage rate in Love Canal—my chance of a miscarriage—was thirty-five to forty-five percent. When the residents who were sitting there heard this, they began yelling. If the percentage was that high, then why the hell were they still here? Patti Grenzy was crying but determined. She said she was out temporarily, and had no intention of moving back. Someone had mentioned the dioxin findings, and people shouted: "What does that mean? Are we going to be exposed? What are you doing to us? Don't you care? We are people. We didn't ask for this. We are victims. And you're minimizing it! You're playing everything down!"

Marie Pozniak got very upset. She has a severely asthmatic daughter, and other medical problems in her family. She was sitting inches from Axelrod. She stood up and said, "In view of the new dioxin findings, Commissioner Axelrod, does that mean that you are going to relocate my family?" Axelrod just put his head down and held it in his hands. She kept after him, "Answer me! Does that mean you are going to relocate me?" He just hung his head, until she finally told him to pick up his head and answer her, that she wouldn't stop until he answered. He said, "No, we are not going to relocate you, Mrs. Pozniak, in view of the dioxin findings." At that, she picked up Dr. Axelrod's cardboard name tag, ripped the "doctor" part off, and threw it at him. She said he didn't deserve a title like "Doctor" or "Commissioner." She ran to the door, where her husband met her, and they left.

I pulled out the twig I had brought and laid it on the table. I asked him what killed this vegetation around Love Canal. He said he didn't know, but according to the reports he had gotten from the DEC, it was winterkill. I explained to him that this particular branch had died that *spring*. It had grown leaves and the leaves turned brown, curled up, and died. It hadn't been below forty degrees. I asked him to explain that. He said he couldn't explain it, that he didn't know; but he would be willing to investigate, if I wanted him to.

The residents, once again, became excited. Everything was chaotic. It was like an opera or a musical, with those up front questioning the commissioners like lead singers, and every once in awhile the audience would cry out just as if they were the chorus. At this time, Commissioner Hennessy said: "I am closing the meeting. We are leaving." I looked at him and said, "No. I still have fourteen points to bring up, questions that have not been answered." Commissioner Hennessy said: "I'm sorry, but the meeting is closed. We have a plane to catch." (They had their own plane. They don't use a regular commercial flight.) It was just an excuse; Commissioner Axelrod was telling us too much. They didn't want us to have the information. They all stood up and started to walk away. I just sat there looking at them. I couldn't believe they were leaving. I threw my papers on the desk and said: "Where the hell do you think you're going?" They said that I was welcome to come to Albany and bring up anything I wanted. I could spend as much time as necessary; but they had a plane to catch, and were sorry. I went over to Axelrod. I was tempted to hit one of them. I'm not a violent person, but I could have hit them with no problem. I paced back and forth, I was so angry. Then I walked away.

It was Grace McCoulf's birthday. She typed and did some of the office work. I wasn't in the mood for a birthday party; I wasn't in the mood for anything. I just paced back and forth trying to get my head together, trying to think straight. But the more I thought about it, the angrier I got. Debbie Cerrillo offered me a ride home, but I told her no, I would walk. I needed a brisk walk.

Later, we went to Grace's house and had birthday cake. We barely got through singing Happy Birthday. All of us were so depressed. We had a glass of wine. Then I said I had to go. I couldn't deal with the party. I went home, stamped around and cleaned my house to relieve that nervous, frustrated energy.

Another Trip to Washington

More and more families were evacuated to Niagara University. The air around the canal was horrible. It smelled like a chemical factory. You could barely breathe. The newspapers were carrying stories about soldiers who had been exposed to Agent Orange which contained dioxin, and were coming down years later with cancer. I met Senator Daly and Assemblyman Murphy. They wrote a letter to Governor Carey, requesting that residents of Love Canal who wished to leave be evacuated.

I had planned another trip to Washington. I convinced them to give me a copy before I left so that I could show it to bureaucrats in the federal government who had ignored the situation. They gave me a copy of the letter critical of the federal agencies. I had arranged appointments in Washington and planned to spend a week to contact as many people as I could from as many agencies to seek federal help. It was obvious the state was going to do nothing and we desperately needed something.

In that same week, we had a meeting with the board of education. Ultimately, we had the 93d Street School closed. We received help from Dr. James Dunlap, the school's physician, and from the parents in the neighborhood. It gave me something else to use when I went to Washington the next week—the dioxin findings, people ill, people living outside the area, the miscarriage data, and now a second school closed. I had a lot of ammunition and was hoping to get somewhere. I left on Sunday, September 5, 1979. The sixth was Labor Day. I planned to put my thoughts and notes together, do some sightseeing on the sixth, then get to work on the seventh.

Washington was beautiful, sunny, and warm. I called some friends I had met through Love Canal and asked if they would go sightseeing with me. We saw the Washington Monument and the White House and all the things that typical tourists go to see. But it was so warm that evening, I got a little silly. Part of it was nerves. I was going to meet people I considered high up. I felt intimidated. I decided I would wade across the reflecting pond to cool off. I rolled up my pant legs, but nobody told me the sides of the pool were slanted and slimy. Very ladylike, I stepped into the pond and proceeded to slide on my butt, right into the water, with the fountain spraying over me. I sat there laughing so hard I couldn't get up. My pocketbook and clothing were soaked. All I thought of was the people back home: LOVE CANAL ASSOCIATION PRESIDENT GOES TO WASHINGTON AND PLAYS IN FOUNTAIN! The sides were so slippery that I couldn't get out of the pond. Besides, I was laughing too hard. If anybody I knew saw me, I would have died; but it was fun, and it relieved my tension.

Doug Costle of EPA, Dr. David Rall of the National Institute of Environmental Health Sciences, Dan Dozier who worked with

Patricia Harris (the new Secretary of Health, Education and Welfare), a representative from the Center for Disease Control, Congressman LaFalce, and I met in the congressman's office the following morning. Channel 2 sent a camera team to film me shaking hands with Congressman LaFalce. Some congressmen have terrible offices. You hear dozens of people typing, xeroxing, teletyping, talking back and forth, with books everywhere. I had expected to see a plush office. The inner office, which was LaFalce's office, wasn't much bigger than the other one.

We began to talk. It was a little crowded with all the representatives in there. I tried to explain our situation at Love Canal, that more residents had been evacuated, and they are now staying at motels, because the students had returned to Niagara University. There were ninety-seven families out, which meant hundreds of people were living in motels.

Everyone was appalled. David Rall agreed with everything I said. He also agreed that the residents shouldn't be there. There could be problems with contamination leaving the site. I asked him why his team didn't come in. Why did they refuse? Axelrod told me that the National Institute had been invited to do health studies at Love Canal, and that the institute refused. I asked Rall why. He said he was asked personally to come to Love Canal as a consultant, but that no one had invited the institute to conduct studies. I repeated what Axelrod had said about the invitation. We went back and forth. Somebody wasn't telling the whole truth.

Dan Dozier said: "If this isn't in your department, then what is? You have got to do something for these people. They can't return home. New York State is not going to evacuate them, and they are going to cut off the temporary funds very soon." Doug Costle said he would see what he could do. Dozier said he would see what he could do. Nothing came of the meeting except more federal officials who were aware of the Love Canal situation.

During the week I met with individuals from EPA. I spoke to the person who was in charge of administering the federal funds that paid for the remedial work and some health studies. This official explained that EPA had appropriated a million dollars for the health department to do its work but that the health department had not signed a contract yet. He couldn't figure out why. He thought the health department didn't want EPA looking over their shoulders at the study. I thought that was strange. Why wouldn't New York State accept a million dollars toward funding their health studies? Usually people and government agencies have to knock down doors to get funds.

I also went with Beverly Paigen to see Joe Highland of the Environmental Defense Fund, to see what he could do to help us. Joe talked about writing books, fund-raising, and political strategies. He came up with some great ideas, ideas that might have helped us get out of Love Canal. I was sorry I hadn't contacted him earlier. Beverly didn't understand why I was depressed when I left the office.

I called the White House several times while I was in Washington, trying to arrange a meeting with Mrs. Carter, to speak with her as one mother to another. I didn't succeed. Her secretary said her calendar was full. Once the secretary said Mrs. Carter was giving a party for a foreign diplomat. I tried to explain that the health of 120 families living in motels was more important than entertaining a foreign diplomat. She promised to talk to Mrs. Carter and see what could be arranged. I did see R. D. Folsom, a White House staff member. I told him I had exhausted every avenue of assistance I knew of except the White House. Folsom said he was sorry, but there was nothing he could do. Love Canal didn't fit any category for which there was a policy. He said he would call me back; but I knew from his attitude that nothing would come from it.

When I returned to my hotel room, I stood on the balcony trying to sort things out. Everyone kept saying the State of New York had to initiate a request, and the State of New York said they had made a request. Yet there was little or nothing in writing. My hotel room looked out on the Watergate complex. It suddenly occurred to me that perhaps there was a massive cover-up in the Love Canal situation.

The health department didn't want the EPA looking over its shoulders. Therefore, the department was willing to give up a million-dollar contract. They didn't want the FDAA or the EPA in, so they didn't request their help. They didn't want the National Institute of Environmental Health Sciences to do a study. That didn't make sense because it would have saved New York taxpayers a lot of money if they had. Of course, if the National Institute were doing the studies, New York State couldn't control what the studies showed; it coudn't decide when to make public what the studies showed. But nothing else made sense.

State officials seemed to be minimizing the risks. That seemed to me the logical reason. They did their studies so poorly that none of them would stand up in court. None of them would stand up to scientific criticism. *That* made sense. I could see the flaws, and I was just a housewife with a high school education.

150 Families, $7,500 a Day

By now, there were a hundred fifty families. The motel bill was $7,500 a day, and the state was threatening to throw families out and force them to return home. From one day till the next, the residents did not know where they would be the next morning. Their lives were disrupted, and so were the lives of their children. Love Canal had caused enough anxiety without them having to wonder where they were going to live next.

While I was in Washington, Harry moved our children into the Howard Johnson Motel on Pine Avenue. Michael was worse, and it was a way to minimize his exposure. Marie Pozniak and the others who worked in the office also moved into motels. United Way's office across the street from the canal was closed because their staff became ill from the fumes.

To get some publicity when I returned to Buffalo, I announced that the State had not applied for help they could have gotten. I told the press that I had picked up a few application blanks, which I intended to deliver to Governor Carey. Perhaps he didn't know how to get them.

I wasn't looking forward to going from Howard Johnson's in Washington to Howard Johnson's in Niagara Falls, but it was better than living in our home. No sooner had I arrived at the motel than one of the residents who was allied with the more radical segment of the organization asked if I had had fun in Washington. Did I have a nice vacation at the expense of the association?

All I could think to say was, *Lady, fourteen meetings in four days is not fun, and I am exhausted. The last thing I want to do is listen to you.* But I ignored her and went into the motel room.

It was small, with two beds, a desk, and a dresser along the one wall. It had a bathroom, and cots for the kids. It was so crowded there was hardly room to move. The kids had their toys. Harry set up his CB. The room became a command center. We could stay in touch with residents in other hotels and with people in their cars, in case something happened. The TV was blaring. Everyone wanted to know how I made out in Washington. The press was banging on the door. It was noisy and confusing. I was exhausted. Marie was trying to tell me what was going on, and I just didn't want to hear it. I didn't want to cope with it; I just wanted to lie down and go to sleep. It was four in the morning by the time everybody cleared out of the room and I could settle down and get some sleep.

The next night, I held a meeting with a few people in the motel to discuss what to do next and what we should do about continuing to get certification from physicians, which we needed in order to stay in the motels. It was also necessary to regain our unity. Under the strain, the association was splitting apart; groups were fighting with one another and hurting the association and the neighborhood. I had scheduled the meeting to try and get the residents to agree not to move out of the motels. That was important. The state couldn't continue to pay several thousand dollars a day for motels, although there was a court order that said they had to. It would be very embarrassing if women and children were thrown into jail. We relied on their unwillingness to jail us. It had worked in the past. But not everyone agreed to stick together. Some people affiliated with a church group did not want to. I didn't want to argue strongly because the group was in danger of splitting up. I didn't want to make people choose sides either. I told everyone to make their own decisions, that it was up to them as individuals to decide what they wanted to do.

Some of the ecumenical task-force members were in the hallway. I tried to explain to them that they should be helping us, and not trying to take over or plan strategy. They didn't understand. We continued to have difficulty with them for some time as they competed with us for leadership in the community.

Albany: "Go Home and Tend Your Garden"

At the task-force meeting in August, David Axelrod said I could come to Albany and he would answer my questions. I decided to go. Of course, I informed the press. When I arrived, there were a number of press and TV people in the outer office.

I talked to them for a few moments, then Axelrod invited me in. Dr. Haughie and Dr. Vianna were there. The office was large and sunny, with many plants. Axelrod asked me why I had come to Albany, and I told him I had written it all in a letter. We began by talking about the women who wanted to have children. Why had nothing been done? Why was he ignoring the problem? He said it was a policy decision, that there was nothing he could do. He only made recommendations. I asked Axelrod what his recommendation was. He wouldn't say at first, but I kept prodding and pushing. Finally, he said he had recommended against relocating women who were contemplating pregnancy. I was shocked. I have often said that nothing about Love Canal would shock me, and then something like this would happen. A health commissioner who knew the miscarriage rate was far above normal, who knew the first trimester of pregnancy was the most delicate time, refused to recommend relocation for those who wished to have more children. It was incredible.

I knew that the press were waiting outside. I could see Dr. Axelrod's public information officer make signs to him when I spoke too loudly. When we talked about the miscarriage data and I asked to see the other studies, Dr. Vianna seemed nervous. He was a chain smoker, and his ashes fell on Axelrod's desk and on the carpet. Vianna couldn't sit still; he kept pacing back and forth. Finally he asked me what the hell I was going to do with his data. Why didn't I go home? I said he was quite correct—that I wasn't a scientist, that I would love to go home—if I had a home that was clean enough to go to. He lit another cigarette, although he had one in the ashtray. He kept pacing up and down and looking out the window; but the only thing he could see out the window was another building. Finally, Dr. Haughie turned around and said: "Why *don't* you go home and tend to your garden?" I was really upset with him. They had told us not to eat food from our gardens. They showed me some tables of data, but they wouldn't let me take anything away. They said everything would be published soon. (It still hasn't.)

We left Axelrod's office about two. The press was waiting. They asked Axelrod what the meeting was about, what his reaction was. He said he thought it was a good meeting, that we communicated very well, that he was very pleased with the meeting. I just made a face. One reporter caught my expression and said: "Mrs. Gibbs' face sure doesn't say that, Commissioner Axelrod. How come she's doing that?" He had nothing to say. I said that I thought it had been a terrible meeting, that I had received absolutely nothing, that I knew no more then than I did when I walked in.

Afterward, I went to the governor's office. I had been trying to see Governor Carey, but I was refused. I met with Jeff Sachs, an aide. He started talking about what a wonderful governor we had, and what a wonderful New York State Health Department we had. So why was I mistreating the governor? Sachs said the governor had been good to us, but the South Bronx had a real problem that is being ignored. Love Canal wasn't the only place in the State of New York that had a problem. By then, I had had it. I finally said, "Jeff, SHUT UP! I have 150 residents sitting in motels. I have 150 residents who are willing to be arrested, who may be carrying shotguns, who are going to sit there and not leave the motel even if the state cuts off the funds. They aren't going to subject their families to dangerous chemicals. Since people had been living in the motels, they felt better. My own son, Michael, used to wet the bed regularly at home but he wasn't doing it in the motel. I also told Sachs that none of the residents would return home, that they were ready to be arrested—men, women, children, and babies—and that it would look bad for both the governor and the State of New York. The residents and I felt a kinship with the boat people escaping from Vietnam. So we called ourselves the "Motel People." Sachs was quiet for the first time in the year and a half that I had known him. He said he sympathized and shook his head. He knew I was serious. He knew the residents were serious. And he knew it would have serious consequences for the State of New York and for Governor Carey. I said I had gone to the FDAA. They said they needed a request from the state. I went to the EPA, and they needed a request from the state. I went to all the other federal Agencies. They all needed the request from the state. Why didn't Governor Carey act? I brought a form from the Federal Disaster Aid Administration for him to fill out and see if he could get federal assistance.

Sachs told me they had already filled out the form. "No, you haven't," I said. I had asked the FDAA, and they said they had received no such request. Sachs didn't say anything. It was strange. He had always been very talkative. He just hung his head or shook his head. We were in a small room. The receptionist kept coming in and giving me messages from the reporters outside. They knew I had gone into the governor's office. Sachs still sat there. He said nothing. Finally, he said he had to go to a meeting but that he would relay the message to the governor.

I was to meet Senator John Daly at his office at four o'clock which gave me a free half-hour. I walked around the State Capitol

Building. It was beautiful—all the sculpture and the winding stair-case. I enjoyed looking at the old building, at the decorations, and the decor. I told Senator Daly what I had been doing. He asked me what I thought would happen. I said the residents would not leave the motels. He wanted to know what could be done to alleviate the situation. I said, temporary relocation now and permanent relocation as soon as possible. I knew that he had been working with Assemblyman Matt Murphy on the bill and both men had been very supportive.

Meeting Jane Fonda

The New York Public Interest Research Group had arranged for Jane Fonda to speak on environmental issues and the toxic waste problem in Niagara County and in Niagara Falls. They asked me if I would invite her to Love Canal. I said I would welcome it. I went to Buffalo with Harry to join her bus tour of the area. The press was there. I had a windowshade that said, Carey-O-Gram. I wanted signatures to support Daly's and Murphy's legislation.

When they had tested the microphone, I asked if I could use it to ask people to sign our windowshade. Steve Vitoff told me that Jane Fonda's plane was late. It was cold and windy, and I was freezing. There were 200 to 250 people on the steps of City Hall. While we were waiting, Vitoff introduced me.

I was desperately trying to talk and stretch it out as long as I could. Then a taxi drove up with Jane Fonda and Tom Hayden in it. I stopped in midsentence. They addressed the crowd, and then we got on the bus for the trip to Love Canal. Jane sat in the second seat with Tom and I sat in the front seat alone. I told them about the plight of the people at Love Canal, and some of the tragic stories of Love Canal families. She is a very caring person and her tears were real. There were no members of the press on the bus, no audience—just she and I talking, and her husband listening, in a bus where no one else could see. She asked a lot of questions, and I gave her all the information I could.

When we arrived at the canal, Jane and Tom Hayden spoke to the crowd. Afterward, we had lunch in the association's office. Keith Gemerek had proudly fixed lunch—he had cooked lunch for Jane Fonda! He smiled every time someone took a second helping. Photographers came in and took pictures of Jane and me eating lunch. Later, when she left for Albany, she took our window-shade with her.

I got permission from the state to tour the canal itself, inside the fence. We showed Jane the boarded up houses, the dead vegetation, the remedial construction. By the time we had finished, it was an emotional scene. Jane Fonda was crying, and Tom Hayden was crying. Both of their staff people and Debbie Cerrillo were crying. Debbie and I put our arms around each other and walked back to the house. I planned on going to Tom's and Jane's cocktail party later that evening but first I had some domestic chores. I had to arrange for the children—pick them up from school and give them a little bit of my time. It was important, to them and me.

I took Keith with me as my escort. He was thrilled over the whole thing. For awhile we mingled with the crowd, eating hors d'oeuvres and talking to people. Jane Fonda and Tom Hayden finally arrived, and we greeted each other. Tom and Jane went up on the stage to speak. They invited me to sit with the speakers on the stage. Both of them talked for awhile. Suddenly a man came out of the blue, cursing and swearing and overturning tables. He went to Ken Sherman, the head of NYPIRG, with a berry pie and smacked it right in his face! There was chaos. People stood up, screaming and hollering, and Ken stood there with pie dripping off his face. He tried to explain why it had happened. Someone told him to wipe the pie off his face first, but he said, "No, that's OK." He talked with pie dripping off the end of his nose. Jane Fonda took a tablecloth from one of the tables and wiped his face. He continued to talk, explaining that a food cooperative in Buffalo was upset with NYPIRG. Afterward, I thanked everyone for the funds some of which were going to our association. I thanked Tom and Jane for coming and supporting us. That was the end of the evening, and we went home.

I think the day was successful despite some of the problems. I thought highly of Jane Fonda and Tom Hayden and enjoyed meeting them. There was one sad note on this day, however. It had been exactly a year since the Kennys lost their son. It was in the back of our minds, and it was mentioned at the rally. It reminded us all of why we were fighting.

Governor Carey: "No Further Relocation"

While all this was going on, sometime during the day, Governor

Carey made an announcement that there would be no further relocation. I thought it was a hopeful sign. The governor could no longer ignore us. We were making so much noise, he had to acknowledge us, even if only to say he was *not* going to do anything. Although some residents were depressed about everything, I was hopeful he would change his mind, if only we kept up the fight.

We had to rely on the media to keep our story alive, and we took advantage of every opportunity. Dr. Janette Sherman, a toxicologist and a physician, was to be an expert witness for us. She flew in from Hawaii. We gave her a tour of Love Canal. Steven Lester, our on-site toxicological consultant, showed her the construction and explained how the containment system would work. We described the residents' reactions during construction. As a result Dr. Sherman wrote a letter to the EPA, saying that the residents of Love Canal should be evacuated, that she was distressed by the way the construction was carried out and by the poor safety precautions that exposed the residents to contaminated air. We released her letter to the press. It created a little more pressure on Albany and a little more of a stir in Washington. Dr. Sherman had a strong reputation as a scientist, and what she said mattered.

The congressional Subcommittee on Oversight and Investigation released its report about this time. The report recommended relocation for residents living in wet areas, at least temporarily, until health and environmental studies would be completed. It criticized David Axelrod and the health department and supported all we were fighting for.

While I was in Washington on still another trip, Governor Carey came to Buffalo. Joanna Hale, one of the residents, read a statement right on the street, asking Governor Carey to purchase our homes at fair market value. I don't know what prompted him to say it, but Governor Carey said the state would buy more Love Canal homes outside rings one and two. Nobody knew what this meant, though. Still, the thought that the state would buy more homes was stunning. I flew home from Washington to find out what was going on.

The following evening we attended a prayer service at a church downtown, organized by the Ecumenical Task Force. The theme was "Let my people go." It was very appropriate and very moving. Norman Kenny sang "Let my people go." Each person read part of the prayer. It brought us together. We joined hands and hopes and prayed that Governor Carey would do what was just and right—which was that all the residents who wanted to leave the area would be allowed to go.

That week, I received a letter from Mrs. Carter's secretary. She declined an invitation to visit Love Canal or to meet with us. The White House had done everything it could. She was busy helping the Vietnam Boat People.

The bill to help the residents of Love Canal went before the state legislature. We were desperately hoping it would pass. And it finally did—almost unanimously (there was only one negative vote). Matt Murphy called me from Lockport, and said it had passed. We were all very, very happy. Everyone with homes in the area from the west side of 93d to 103d, and bordered by the Creek and Buffalo Avenue, would be relocated.

I couldn't believe it: we had actually won our major goal—permanent relocation. People went out and bought champagne. The media flocked in. Everyone was laughing, joking, very happy. But still, we had been disappointed many times before. When TV reporters asked us how we felt, we all said Hurrah! Someone poured champagne over my head. It was a great feeling to see those people so happy. One reporter said the "little people" had finally won. I corrected him: "We are not *little people*. We are the *big people* who vote them in. We have the power, they don't!"

The evening went quickly. We celebrated, but it was to prove premature. Our stay at the motel ended November 5, 1979, but there was still no resolution of the relocation plans. We didn't know when we would be able to move. After the governor's announcement, we debated whether we would try to stay in the motels until we were actually relocated. But people believed the governor would follow through; and besides they were tired.

It was an eerie feeling when I walked into our house. I felt as if I didn't belong there. It was cold, dangerous, and very frightening. It wasn't my house anymore.

A revitalization committee was formed to appraise houses and purchase them. They called it "revitalization" because they were interested in bringing new families into this unsafe area. The committee was composed entirely of officials. An advisory committee would represent the community, but it had little or no say. The mayor chaired the committee. For some time, the revitalization committee did nothing but try to organize itself. Eventually, it did get organized, but then it turned out they couldn't spend the state's money without matching federal money; and those

funds didn't come until just before election day in November
1980.

We checked the pregnancies that occurred in the last year at
Love Canal. Out of fourteen pregnancies, we found only two that
resulted in normal births. The rest were stillborns or miscarriages.
One poor child was born with his diaphragm and intestines outside
his body. He had six operations and died in September 1980.
Some had such birth defects as clubfoot and six toes. The fetus is
a sensitive indicator. What was happening to babies that were
being conceived and carried at Love Canal showed the potential
and actual damage to our children and to us.

I made this survey public to reinforce our statements about
the health hazards here and to emphasize that the area should not
be revitalized. People should no longer be living there. Once that
was made public, the press called the health department for a
response. The health department had no data. They had done no
follow-up studies! They had not followed the pregnancies in the
area. And they are the professional scientists charged with
guarding public health. The health department wanted me to
identify the women for them. I refused, saying the department
had not given me the information I requested. Therefore, I would
not share any data with them. They tried going through the
Niagara County Medical Society. I received a letter from the
society asking for the names. I asked one of the health department officials why they wanted it. It was only "useless housewife data." That is what they told me about our other study, so
why should this one be any different?

I continued to stay in contact with Jane Fonda, and also
with Henry Fonda, trying to get *60 Minutes* to do a story on Love
Canal. Mike Wallace said he could not do an environmental toxic-
waste story; but we wanted him to cover Beverly Paigen's story.
Dr. Paigen had been harassed by the New York State Health
Department because she was involved in the Love Canal problem.
David Axelrod delayed approval of a contract for her laboratory.
He and others tried various ways to make it difficult for her to
operate the lab. Because she was helping people and because she
disagreed with official policy, she got into difficulty. What has
happened to democracy? What has happened to our God-given
rights? A good scientist like Beverly is harassed because she is
doing something for the community. No wonder we had difficulty finding others to help.

David Axelrod surprised me. He is a respected scientist. I

always thought that when he became commissioner, we would have a chance. But the position made it difficult for him to separate science from politics. He couldn't hold his head up straight or look us in the eye when he talked with us. If I've learned anything from this experience, it's that science is not separate from politics, no matter how much the scientists pretend it is.

Chromosome Studies

Late Friday afternoon, May 16, 1980, marked the beginning of the end of our struggle. Both kids had gone to Burger King with grandma and the house was unusually quiet. Even the phone wasn't ringing. Taking advantage of this rare moment of quiet, I ran a full tub of hot water, planning to soak in the bath for an hour. I took the phone into the bathroom with me because my phone was never silent for as long as an hour. I got in the tub and relaxed. It felt good.

The phone rang. I let it ring a few times while I wiped my arm dry. Then I picked up the receiver. The cheery voice of a stranger asked me how I was doing. I felt like telling him I had been doing fine until he called.

He identified himself as a representative of the EPA. He had the results of the chromosome studies they had done on thirty-six Love Canal residents. The EPA wanted to speak with each person tomorrow at Love Canal to discuss individual results. They were going to fly in doctors who could properly explain what the results meant. He wanted me to notify the thirty-six families and set up appointments from eight in the morning until noon.

I said the government must be crazy. What was the hurry! Why couldn't it wait till Monday? He then told me that someone had leaked the results to the press and they wanted to talk to the people who had been tested as soon as possible. God, that made me mad! Every time a government agency does something, the press got the results before we did.

The EPA official read off names and phone numbers to me. I was still in the tub soaking wet, with nothing to write with but a bar of soap and a bathroom wall. I told him to wait a minute while I got a pen and paper. I wrote down the names and numbers of the people involved and called Marie, our office manager, for help. She came right over. I called the first two people. They agreed to come in the next day; but they insisted that I knew the results and wouldn't tell them. It took twenty-five to thirty minutes with each before I could get off the phone. I asked Marie to call someone else to help her, knowing it would take us all night to do it at thirty minutes a call.

By eight o'clock, we had reached thirty-four of the thirty-six families. The other two had gone camping for the weekend. By then the news had gotten around. The house was filled with people, and the phone never stopped ringing. It's hard to believe that just a few hours ago I was relaxing.

There was no need to set the alarm clock that Saturday morning. Reporters started calling me at 5:30 to get a story in time for the morning edition. I had hardly gotten to the office when people began to arrive—news reporters, EPA representatives, residents, doctors. Within fifteen minutes there were twenty-five people, all talking loudly. TV camera lights were turned on and off throughout the building. The EPA officials were trying to figure out how they could conduct private interviews in the midst of this circus. I ignored the craziness long enough to finish putting on my make-up and grab a cup of coffee. This was going to be a *long* day!

As I came out of the bathroom, about eight people yelled "Lois" at the same time. No one else was doing it, so I took charge. I asked Debbie to throw the press out. Boy! Were they angry at me! I then asked the residents to wait in the kitchen and the EPA representatives to meet in my office.

We found space for each of the EPA doctors to speak privately with the families. Dr. Paigen was good enough to remain in the kitchen with the families, to answer questions about their test results. She has been so good to us. She was always around when we needed her, always willing to give herself to help us.

The EPA had set aside a half-hour for each family with one of their doctors to explain the results and answer questions. The atmosphere in the office that day was strange. The residents who were waiting were quiet. They were frightened and depressed. The newspaper reports said that eleven of the thirty-six residents tested showed broken chromosomes of a rare type. Each one who heard the news believed that they were one of the eleven. According to the news stories, the chromosome breaks meant an increased risk of miscarriages, stillborns, birth defects, cancer, or genetic damage, which could affect their children's children. The thought of cancer or genetic damage, understandably, frightened people. Some arrived at the office crying. Others were so nervous they couldn't sit; they just paced back and forth. There wasn't much small talk.

You could feel the tension mounting. When the first families were called in to see the doctors, a cold chill ran down my back. The first family came out after their interview. The couple just stood in the doorway, not saying a word. Then they slowly walked over to Dr. Paigen and began to cry. The room became silent. The woman told Beverly that the doctors handed her and her husband a piece of paper with numbers on it, then told them that both had an abnormal number of breakages, and, as if that weren't bad enough, the breakages were of a rare type. EPA doctors couldn't tell them what that meant to their family. All the doctors would say was that the test results were only an indication of health risks in a population. No one could say what the result meant in any individual case. When the woman asked about the effects on her children, she was told that if her breakage and that of her husband were due to exposure to Love Canal chemicals, and the children were also exposed, the chances were good that the children also had chromosome breaks. There was nothing they could do as parents except move their children away from Love Canal.

As the woman spoke about her children, she became even more upset. If they could have afforded to move out, she said, they would have moved a year ago! Her husband put his arm around her and took her home. As they were leaving, she looked back at the closed door where the EPA doctors were speaking with another couple and yelled "Damn you, EPA! Damn you, stupid government!"

As soon as the couple stepped out of the door, at least twenty reporters from all over the country encircled them. That poor woman. She had enough to deal with without trying to answer their questions!

While I was looking out the window, an angry yell came from upstairs. The family was shouting at an EPA official. The official went upstairs to tell them that their half-hour was up. They would have to leave because other people were waiting to talk to the doctor. The family was telling him to go to hell! They were going to talk to the doctor until *all* their questions are answered. It was just too bad about their schedule!

Government officials are terribly insensitive! I wondered whether, if he were in that family's position, he would leave because his "time was up!" Some government people are so unfeeling.

They are nothing but machines.

In December, when they drew blood for the tests, the EPA representative in charge of the project stood at the door where the blood was being taken and said to each person as they left, "Thank you for your blood." It was as if the EPA official were running a blood bank for Count Dracula. At the time I thought it was funny. Now I can see with how little feeling government officials have treated us, from the very beginning.

The tension in the office increased as people went in and out of doctors' rooms. Most of the families were as confused when they came out as when they went in. Tempers grew shorter; people were visibly upset. Even those families with negative findings were upset, wondering whether they had been told the truth or whether their children might yet be affected. Beverly was great. She was there to try to answer the residents' questions. Debbie kept throwing out media people trying to get in. I tried to keep things running as smoothly as best I could, but it was difficult to keep from being deeply moved by my friends' tears and their shock. I kept wondering how much more those people could take! One of these days, they will go crazy, I thought.

There was a noon press conference in Congressman LaFalce's Niagara Falls office. Then I understood why the doctors put such tight time limits on their interviews.

About a hundred residents showed up for the press conference, including the mayor, Congressman LaFalce, and EPA doctors and officials. They announced the results to the press and answered a few questions. The most frequent question was: "Are you going to move the residents of Love Canal, based on this information?" They said they didn't know. They would have the answer the first part of the next week.

After the press conference the mayor, who was so angry at the EPA for the way they handled this release, grabbed the main EPA official and pushed him against a wall. "You can't drop this bomb in my city then walk out, leaving me with this mess!" the mayor screamed. It looked funny. The EPA representative was well over six feet tall and the mayor looked like a child having a temper tantrum.

Taking Hostages

When we opened the office Monday morning, it didn't take long before it was filled with residents, reporters, and other interested people. There were many rumors about what the federal government would do. Everyone was anxious and full of questions. I spent most of my day on the phone or in front of a TV camera. In the early afternoon someone showed me a newspaper headline reading: WHITE HOUSE BLOCKS LOVE CANAL EVACUATIONS. Everyone around me was angry, upset, cursing, and swearing. A few began to cry, saying, "What the hell do they need, dead bodies in the streets?" Everyone was sure we would be evacuated. The headline shocked us.

Word spread quickly through the neighborhood. People gathered on the lawn in front of the Homeowners Association office. As people talked to each other, they became angrier and angrier. There were about fifty people out front when I decided I had to give them a target for their anger. But I had no idea what would be best. I went out and began to talk with the people. In a few minutes the crowd grew from fifty people to almost 100, with more coming. The crowd became louder and disorderly. Someone poured gasoline on a lawn across the street, forming the letters EPA; then they put a match to it. The flaming letters drew loud applause and cheers from the crowd.

A woman who had had several miscarriages and had a child born with a birth defect, broke down. She couldn't take any more. She stopped a car that was coming down the street and asked the driver if he lived on Love Canal? When he said no, that he was going to the mall to shop, she told him he had better take another route. Crying all the while, she told him that her family was going to die in Love Canal because no one would help her. "This area is condemned, and we'll die alone. No one who does not live in the neighborhood is allowed in. Go another way to the mall." Because she was so upset, she yelled at the driver. People overheard what she said, and they supported her. They gathered in the street and stopped every car that tried to get through. It wasn't long before the police arrived and told us to get out of the street or we would be arrested.

I was as angry as the other residents. I told one police officer to arrest me. I didn't care. I was so upset, I couldn't think straight. I can't remember being this angry any time during the past two years. I guess I knew this was it. If they didn't evacuate us then, they never would! I wouldn't have taken much to start crying, I was so frustrated! But because I was president of the association, I had to be strong and positive. I had to do something to keep our hopes alive.

I was afraid people were going to tear the neighborhood apart. Everyone was cursing EPA, discussing the chromosome study and what the study actually meant. I decided to bring the EPA officials to the office. I hoped the residents would focus their anger on them. They needed a target to vent their frustrations. Attacking innocent passerbys or police officers who were trying to do their jobs could only hurt our cause.

I knew that two EPA representatives were somewhere in Niagara Falls, a doctor and a public relations man. Supposedly, they were left behind to answer residents' questions when the rest returned to Washington. But no one bothered to tell us where they were staying or how to contact them. I went back into the office and started calling every motel. I finally reached Frank Napal, the PR man, and explained the situation. He agreed to come to the office and talk to the residents.

I went out and told the residents that the EPA representatives were on their way. The residents could ask what was going on or raise any questions they might have about the chromosome study. The sun was warm on my face as I sat on the steps waiting. In front of me was the burned grass spelling "EPA." The residents were in little groups, talking. Some were aimlessly walking back and forth in the road and stopping cars that came into the neighborhood. As I was sitting there, I thought: *What a mess this is! Why did I ever move to this neighborhood? When will it be over? If one more reporter asked me a question, I was going to scream!*

My reverie of feeling sorry for myself was interrupted when I heard one of the residents saying we should take the EPA representatives hostage. "Let's see how much they like being in this neighborhood. If we can't leave, and we have to die here, then they can, too!" The other residents agreed that it was a good idea. Within minutes, the idea spread through the crowd, and as if the crowd was a single mind, everyone decided to hold the EPA officials hostage when they arrived. By now there were about 300 people out front. As they talked to one another they stimulated each other's anger.

When the EPA's public relations representative arrived, the crowd suddenly became silent. He introduced himself as a public relations man, not a doctor. He said the doctor was at the motel near a phone, should a resident call for information. "How can anyone call him when no one knows where he is?" I told him to look outside. "If you dare to go out there and tell these people you can't answer their questions because you are not a doctor, they'll lynch you. Believe me, you won't get out alive! Those people are *mad!* You better get on the phone and get that doctor here fast!"

Napal picked up the phone to call the doctor. At that point, one of the women asked me if we were holding him hostage. I sidestepped her question and told her he was calling the doctor, who might be able to answer some of our questions. I am afraid I was a little short with her because I was so angry. The tension was really building—in the office and in the street. It was as though I were listening to a bomb ticking, waiting for it to explode. Some people were throwing gasoline on trees and signs and lighting them. Others were beating their fists on cars entering the neighborhood and yelling at the drivers. The city police were everywhere, and reporters and cameras were scattered throughout the crowds. More and more people arrived. I was afraid the situation was getting out of control. No one was thinking with a clear head, and I was afraid I wouldn't be able to reason with them. I'm not sure even I had a clear head. I was as angry as they were! I *was not* going to take my children back to our house on 101st Street. It wasn't safe! I had almost lost Missy a few months ago because of a blood disorder, and I didn't want to go through that again!

The doctor finally arrived and went directly into the office. I think he was a little frightened of the crowd. He no sooner introduced himself than yells could be heard from outside. "We have them!" "Let's see how they like being trapped here!"

I looked at both and told them that they were hostages of the "Love Canal People." I told them no harm would come to them, but that if they left the office, I could not be responsible for what the crowd, now numbering nearly 500 people, would do. We had no guns, no other weapons; but for their own protection, I advised them to stay in our office. We had plenty of food, all homemade, and they could use the phone as they wished. My office was so packed with reporters and residents, no one could walk through it. I had no idea of what one did when holding hostages. I thought to myself: *Why didn't I watch TV more carefully!*

It wasn't hard to figure out that we should tell someone, never thinking the press was already telling the whole world. I decided to call the White House. I knew I would never be able to talk to the President, and I didn't want to talk to a lackey. So I put in a call to Jack Watson. He was President Carter's chief of

staff and had been involved in Love Canal on and off since 1978.
I went into the hall (I couldn't hear myself think in my crowded
office) and called Watson. His secretary answered. I said: "My
name is Lois Gibbs, president of the LCHA, in Niagara Falls, New
York. The Love Canal residents are holding two EPA officials
hostage. I would like to speak to Mr. Watson about this matter."
I was trying to sound calm and objective, not easy under the circumstances. The secretary in a very mechanical voice said,
"Would you hold, please, Mrs. Gibbs?" She asked me to hold
when I told her we were holding federal officials hostage!

In a few moments, she said she would deliver my message to
Watson. She went on to say that we were wrong, that we should
let the EPA officials go, adding: "You people have blown Love
Canal all out of proportion. I have friends who have cancer and
they don't live at Love Canal and . . . . "

I told her to go to hell! Then I asked her if she personally
took care of Watson's business. Did she run the White House?
Thank God, I wasn't a crazy or I might have shot the EPA officials
in reaction to her arrogant comments. It was hard to believe the
White House had such an insensitive person on its staff. No
wonder we couldn't get any help with people like that working for
the government. Her statements must also have reflected atti-
tudes in the White House.

The office was a three-ring circus. It was so hot, one could
hardly move or breathe. I stood on a chair and announced that I
had called the White House. I asked every one to leave the room
and I would make an announcement from the porch out front in a
few minutes. The room cleared out except for a few residents
who stayed while I went out front to speak to the crowd. I tried
to quiet the crowd (there was no PA system). My voice isn't
very loud. As people moved in toward the porch, I noticed beer
bottles on the ground and many teenagers in the crowd. Beer
and teenagers meant trouble.

When the crowd quieted down, I said I had notified the
White House that the officials were being held hostage by the Love
Canal residents. The crowd cheered. Then I said, "I don't know
what Washington is going to do, but I expect a call back soon." I
stressed that they should stay calm and orderly. "We have not
been destructive or violent in the past. Let's not do it now. As
soon as I hear something, I'll tell you." I restricted the building to
no more than five people at a time and only one person from the
media at a time. That would ensure the safety of the hostages.

The crowd was hostile: "They ain't ensuring our safety. Why should we ensure theirs?" and: "To hell with them! Let them suffer just like we have the past two years!" I had forgotten for a moment how touchy the crowd was; but they reminded me quickly enough.

I went back into the office and asked everyone to leave. I let Marie Pozniak decide who would stay. Marie knew just about everyone in the neighborhood because she dealt with them every-day. She knew who could be counted on to remain level-headed in a crisis.

Back in the office, I suddenly realized what we had done. The news reporters asked me if I were worried about going to jail. I told them I wasn't doing anything wrong. I was protecting the EPA officials from the crowd. I realized that there were too many people in the room who should not be held responsible, so I asked everyone except Barbara Quimby to leave. I asked her if she would stay even if it meant she could go to jail. She said she felt safer in here than out in that crowd. She was willing to do whatever was necessary to help her children. She stood guard at the door to make sure neither residents nor the press entered without our permission and to see that the EPA officials didn't leave.

The last of the residents and the press had left. There were just the four of us. Things quieted down in the rest of the building. Marie successfully ushered people out. I apologized to the hostages, telling them we were sorry they were taking the heat for the big shots in Washington sitting in plush offices.

Barbara's husband knocked on the door. She was afraid he was going to pull her out; but to her surprise, he didn't. They spoke very softly. Jim asked her if she knew what she was doing. She said she knew and that she was doing it for her children. "Please understand, Jim." He looked at her for a second. Then he told her to do what she felt she had to do, that he loved her and was proud of her. He said he would be outside the door if she needed him.

Not long after he closed the door, we heard a man's voice shouting. I couldn't make out what he was saying. I hoped Marie had posted large people at the door! At first, I couldn't tell who it was, but then my heart sank and I recognized the voice. The person hated me and the association. He repeatedly accused us of holding secret meetings with officials. He could not be described as cool and collected; in fact he was just the opposite.

Marie told us he was outside and her "guards wouldn't let

him in." He was accusing us of holding a secret meeting with EPA. She said he had gone off again and was furious. She no sooner closed the door than there was a crash. The window next to me splattered in a thousand pieces. I was as frightened as everyone else in the room. I looked around to see if anyone was hurt. Jim Quimby came charging through the door to see what happened. Our hostages, sensing the crowd's mood, were becoming edgy themselves.

Out front people seemed to be milling around confused. I had no idea if someone shot at the window or threw something or what happened! One of the residents pushed through the hedge outside and poked his head into the space where the window once was. He asked if everyone was all right. He explained that the person thought we were holding a secret meeting and put his arm through the window. He said that the man cut his elbow but that he would be OK.

I asked the resident to get some strong men outside the windows and doors. I turned back to see one of the hostages helping clean up the glass. He was holding the dust pan while Barbara's husband swept the pieces into it. For some reason, that struck me funny. He looked as if he belonged with us, not as though he was being held against his will. Unfortunately, the other man was not as calm. He looked white. He sat there as if he were waiting for something horrible to happen to him.

I explained to both hostages that everything was under control. People were guarding the windows and doors to protect them. I said that to try to reassure them, especially the one who was so frightened.

The phone rang. It was Chuck Warren, from the EPA regional office in New York City. He wanted to know what was going on. I explained about the five hundred angry people out front, the broken window, and the EPA officials whom we were calling hostages to keep the crowd happy. I said that, in all truth, we were protecting them—in hopes they wouldn't arrest us. He asked me to let them go. I reminded him of the crowd and the broken window. I told him it was impossible; they would never make it off the porch before the crowd attacked them. I said that I felt a responsibility to protect people from possible harm, which was more than the government felt toward us.

He asked to talk to Frank, one of the hostages. I sat down to collect my thoughts. I wondered why the White House hadn't called back. Didn't they care that we were holding hostages?

When Frank hung up, the phone rang. It was Congressman LaFalce. He had been fighting as hard as we were to get something done at Love Canal. He was really upset with us! He told me to let the hostages go, that he had a lot of respect for me and thought I was a credit to the community, a fair person, and one whom he felt he could always deal with openly. But this hostage business surprised him. He said he was doing everything he could to help us and was going to meet with President Carter later that evening. He would convey our problem to the President himself. I told him I couldn't let them go! He explained how something that starts innocently can turn into a disaster. That could happen here. We were asking for real trouble if we continued. I knew he was right. The beer bottles, the teenagers, the broken window, the crowd's angry yells—all that flashed through my mind as he was talking.

But we had gone too far to turn back. It's "do or die," and we felt we would die if we didn't get help!

The crowd seemed to be growing. There were many unfamiliar faces. There could be trouble we might not be able to control. Love Canal residents are law-abiding citizens. I felt they would listen to me. But outsiders, that was another matter. Protests bring out some strange people, as we had found out on other occasions.

The crowd was restless. They needed something. I went out again to let them know what was happening. Talking, communicating with the people was the best, even if you don't have much to say. I walked out on the porch and asked the people to quiet down. In the back of my mind I thought, *What am I going to tell you people?* I couldn't tell them the White House hadn't even bothered to call back! That Washington did not care!

I said I had talked with Congressman LaFalce and that he would be meeting with the President for dinner that evening. He would tell the President we were holding hostages at Love Canal. The crowd cheered long and loud. When they quieted again, I told them that Congressman LaFalce asked that we release the hostages. I said that so the EPA officials would hear it. "No," shouted the crowd in unison. I told them that as long as they voted "No," we would continue. But we needed blankets, food, and coffee if we were going to continue to hold them. That gave the crowd something to do, a way to participate. I went back into the office.

Rich Lippes and his partner wanted me to let the EPA people

go. Every time I referred to the EPA representatives as "hostages," they told me *not* to use that phrase. It could cost me five years in prison! I don't think even our attorneys understood how desperate we were! Nothing we had done had gotten us out. Our children were sick and our homes were worthless. It was dangerous to become pregnant. And now we were told of possible genetic damage. How much can human beings take without rebelling? Even though the attorneys didn't completely understand, they were still on our side, and their presence gave me a little feeling of security.

Poor Barbara Quimby had been alone with the hostages for quite awhile. I left the attorneys and went to relieve her. Barbara can be funny, even without trying because she is so honest, and straightforward and just says what she thinks. Barbara looked at me in the strangest way, gave a sigh of relief, then blurted out she would do anything to get her family out, she would do anything I told her to do; but she was drawing a line. I couldn't figure out what was wrong. The EPA men were quietly reading Love Canal stories in papers and magazines from our files. The crowd had calmed down somewhat. Why was she acting this way?

I asked what was wrong. Pointing to one of the EPA representatives, and talking in a loud voice she said he had to go to the bathroom and she refused to go in the bathroom with him. "I'll do anything Lois, but don't make me watch him go potty!" Before I could answer, she said, "I knew this would happen. I knew one of them would have to go! Good God in heaven, don't make me go!" She was so funny, I couldn't help but laugh. Even the EPA representatives got a kick out of her. I told her it was all right. She didn't have to go. I sent one of the men outside to watch the window, to let the EPA man go to the toilet by himself.

After an hour and a half and no word from Washington, the residents on the street were growing louder. They seemed to be worked up again. It was getting dark. Some of them were drinking beer. I noticed strange faces in the crowd. I couldn't tell whether they were FBI agents, or just curious people and students. I was hoping they weren't troublemakers!

People outside began yelling, "Where's Lois? What's happening?" The FBI called and gave me seven minutes to release the EPA officials or they would rush the crowd. If the FBI had begun pushing through, there would have been a riot. There were women and children in the crowd, and I couldn't let them get hurt at any cost. How could we convince the residents to let the EPA representatives go, yet save face for the association? I decided to go out to the crowd and figure it out as I went along. In the meantime, the FBI gave us a telephone countdown: "You have two minutes!"

I announced that I was going out and talk to my people. We would either release the hostages, or we would be wiping up blood. I walked out on the porch and asked the people to come closer, because I had no PA system. While they gathered around, I thought to myself: *If I say one wrong word, it could be disastrous.* I started out by repeating what I said earlier. "Congressman LaFalce is meeting with the President for dinner. He will tell him our demands and that we are holding hostages at Love Canal." I paused to get my thoughts together. The residents were silent. All you could hear was the clicking and grinding of news and TV cameras. I said that Love Canal people were tired of waiting for government, tired of being told our health was at risk, but that they would do nothing. We had shown them we mean business. We weren't going to put up with any more of their bureaucratic bullshit! There was a lot of yelling and applause at this point. I said that I believed that we had made our point, that President Carter would discuss us at dinner. "It is up to you what we do from here, but I think to continue to hold these two will hurt us more than it will help us." The crowd booed. It was not going over very well. If there was a God and He had a miracle, I sure needed it then.

I continued talking to the residents. "Here is the message we should deliver to Washington. Here are your EPA people. What you have seen us do here today will be a Sesame Street picnic in comparison with what we will do if we do not get evacuated. We want an answer from Washington by noon Wednesday!" The crowd applauded. I asked the residents what they wanted to do. Although the show of hands was about fifty-fifty, I said: "The majority wants to let them go. But remember, we want an answer by noon Wednesday, or this will look like a Sesame Street picnic!"

As I went back in the house, I could hear people say "Lois is a traitor." "I wouldn't let them go." "Why is she chickening out?" I could understand. I'm sure if I didn't know about the FBI, I would probably feel the same way. We told the hostages that they were free to go. There were police everywhere. To ensure their safety, the FBI wanted me to lead them to the police car. Lucky me! I agreed. We left by the back door and we were swamped with reporters. It was almost impossible to walk. Someone kept pushing me, saying, "Don't stop!" The hostages were safe in the car. I returned to the office to look for Barbara. She was gone. Someone said she went in the police car with the EPA guys. We all started to panic. Maybe she had been arrested! She returned a few minutes later. She had been thrown into the police car by mistake and was sitting between the two EPA men. When the officers asked who she was, she looked at the EPA men and prayed they wouldn't identify her. After a slight pause, the EPA men said they didn't know who she was. The officer, after dropping the EPA men off, brought her back to the office. I think the EPA men didn't say anything because all that time Barbara had been giving them Love Canal stories to read and had told them about her own family's problems. Both she and her husband had been told they had broken chromosomes, and they had a retarded child. I believe when they left, they felt sorry for her and the rest of us.

The following morning, I called my attorney to see what was going to happen. He said nothing, if I stayed out of trouble. Thank God!

One special moment was almost lost in the craziness. Two small children, a little boy and girl about seven years old, came to the broken window. The little boy gave me chocolate chip cookies and told me if I went to jail he would write me some letters. The little girl gave me a plastic baggie with cookies, which she was going to eat herself. She told me to take the cookies because they didn't have cookies in jail. She then said she loved me because I was helping her mother. That was touching. I guess that's the real reason why we did fight so hard—for our children.

"My Little Julie Is Dead!"

On May 20 the Niagara County legislators met. They were to vote whether to participate in the revitalization agency that was to be formed to purchase our homes. The agency had only $10 million, about one third of the necessary money. The legislature had tabled a decision twice before. The residents wanted an answer at this meeting. We believed the agency could not be established without their support.

The legislative chamber held about seventy-five people, but that night over two hundred residents came out. The Love Canal people were still excited following the hostage episode. We wore red carnations to symbolize our cause. The room was packed. People spilled out into the hall. With the crowd, the room quickly became very warm and uncomfortable that summerlike evening. TV cameras and newspaper people were out in force. Their bright lights blinded us and added to the temperature. Network TV reporters from around the country were waiting to see what would happen at Wednesday noon. Some of our people were permitted to speak to our issue. I went first. I walked up to the podium and stood there for a minute looking out over the thirty-five male and one female legislators. They sat at neat desks in front of me. The chairman and legislative officers were at my left. I felt as if I were on trial, pleading my case. The cameras circled me. I could barely see the legislators. I asked them to vote yes or no, but for God's sake, make a decision. I asked them to support us as our representatives. My speech was short and to the point.

Five others spoke, pleading with the legislators to support us. Of all the people who spoke, Liz Retton, a Love Canal resident, was the most effective. Her story was carried across the country.

She approached the podium with a speech in her hand, a speech she never read, because she spoke from her heart. She said she was a former resident of Love Canal. She still owned her house on 100th Street, but she had evacuated it on February 8, 1979, under the commissioner's order because she was pregnant with her second child. Liz began to tremble. Her eyes filled with tears. She had moved out temporarily to protect her unborn child and her two-year-old daughter. She carried her baby Julie nine months. Everything seemed to be fine. By now, tears were running down her cheeks. She didn't bother to wipe them. She was in a trancelike state, reliving the birth of her child. Speaking very softly, she said her baby was stillborn, that it was dead. "My little Julie is dead because of Love Canal. Please, I beg you to support the bill tonight before this happens again!" Liz could barely walk away from the podium when she was through, she was crying so hard.

Everyone was touched by her story. The cameras followed her back to her seat. Love Canal residents had tears in their eyes, but our emotions were mixed. We felt frustration—and something near hate.

When everyone was through talking, the legislators voted fifteen for participating and sixteen against. Residents became angry. They shouted at the legislators, calling them names, hooting, shouting, crying, and worse. The crowd was close to riot. The legislators recessed for forty-five minutes in hopes of calming the crowd.

When the legislators returned, I was furious. I stood at the podium and asked if someone would please tell us why they voted against participation in the committee to buy our homes. There was no response. The cameras were all around me, but I couldn't see the legislators. I decided to stand on the chair. Again and again I asked "Why," with no answer. I was asked to leave so they could go on with their business; but I refused until I had an answer to my simple question. An hour went by, with me on the chair and the legislators sitting silently at their desks.

Two police officers said that if I did not get down, they would have to remove me. I told them I was not moving until I got an answer. One of the officers whispered to me that he had just called home to tell his wife he would be late. She asked him to deliver a message to me, thanking me for the overtime, for us to keep up the good work and that she was behind us. That struck me funny. I guess there is some good in even a bad situation. The police offficer who was going to arrest me had a wife sitting at home cheering us on! After awhile, two policemen escorted me out, followed by TV cameras. I was determined to get an answer from the legislators. After the police allowed the TV crews back into the legislative hall, I hid between the TV cameras entering from the main hall. Once inside, I went to the podium and again asked: "Why did you vote no? We want an answer!" It took the legislators by surprise. The residents laughed and cheered.

After fifteen minutes, I was removed again. A police officer was detailed to guard me closely. I was determined to get back in there again. Looking around, I spotted an unguarded side door. I waited until the officer's head was turned and then moved toward the door. Marie Pozniak noticed me slipping into the door and so did the police officer. To give me a head start, Marie goosed the officer. Everyone around laughed, including the officer. I came in the back of the gallery. The legislators were facing the other way, so they did not see me enter. I yelled: "We want an answer from you turkeys! Tell us why!" It startled a few of the legislators. A few of them laughed, but the rest were angry. It was almost 11:00, and they had not yet begun their agenda. I was removed again. On my way out I noticed a side room with peanuts and potato chips on the table. I picked up an armful of goodies on my way out, to pass out to the residents. At 11:00, I

told everyone to go home to their families. There was no use
staying. "We'll get them next election. That's when they'll pay
for this." Everyone was happy to leave. The past two days had
been strenuous. Everyone was tired.

Finally, Relocation

I went home, too—frustrated, exhausted, and worried. The noon
deadline for a response from Washington was only twelve hours
away. If there were no answers, what were we going to do? Was
there anything left except destructive violence? I was too tired
to think and went to bed about 1:30 in the morning. The phone
began to ring at five with reporters wanting to know what I heard
and what we were going to do.

With the residents' mood, I would have no control over the
crowd if anything started. Anything was possible. I must have
talked with fifty reporters that morning before I made it to the
office.

The streets were crowded with people, students, teachers,
media, residents, politicians. There wasn't a parking place within
two blocks of the office. Even getting out of my car was a challenge. Everyone wanted to talk to me. Everyone wanted to know
our plan if nothing happened.

Marie and I went into the back office where it was quiet. I
told her I had no idea what would happen this afternoon, but I
had heard that Washington would make some kind of statement at
noon. Marie really has been great throughout the past two years.
She was willing to do anything to help. She faithfully worked in
the office every day, despite stress and turmoil. She looked very
drawn and nervous this morning, but I was happy she was with
me.

I picked up the phone and began calling one number after
another, trying to get an answer from Washington. As I was
waiting on hold for another official, I stared out the window. It
was a warm, sunny spring day. The buds on the trees were just
opening, showing small green leaves. The children were riding
bicycles up and down the streets. People were gathered in small
groups talking to one another, some holding babies. Reporters
were milling through the crowd, asking questions, positioning
people for their cameras. Trucks and cars with the stations' names
written on them were lined up at the curbs. It was much too nice
a day to be ruined by an unhappy ending.

At 11:00, a group of reporters got into the office and de-manded to know our plans. I told them all I knew, that the EPA would provide a press release at noon in Washington. I called the EPA press officer. She said I would have to wait until noon along with everyone else. The rest of the world didn't have hundreds of residents waiting anxiously and the media badgering them.

At 11:45, I went outside. Someone set up a chair by the office window and placed the phone on the window sill. At one minute to 12:00 the phone rang. Twenty microphones were in front of my face. I could hardly see beyond the cameras, the microphones, and the TV lights. A hush fell over the crowd. I said "Love Canal Homeowners Association. Lois Gibbs speaking." It was a news reporter who wanted to know what was happening! I firmly but politely told him that if he wanted to know, he should get off his butt like the rest of the reporters and come down to the office. No releases over the phone! Those in the crowd who heard me chuckled. People started moving, shifting their positions. Five after twelve and still no call. I called the press office back myself.

The press receptionist at first refused to read the press release to me, but when I insisted she found someone to read it. I an-nounced that I would repeat the press statement as it was read to me, so we could all hear it together. I was desperately hoping it would be good news. The press statement began with an overview of the problems, the chromosome-breakage study, and, of course, their concern for the residents. While the woman was reading to me and I was repeating the statements to the crowd, you could hear the sounds of dozens of cameras. The residents were silent, almost as if the crowd was holding its breath, waiting for the answer. Personnel from the New York State office across the street came out to hear what was being said.

Then the woman read what we all wanted to hear. I was just in ecstasy as I heard her say that eight hundred and ten families in the Love Canal community would be evacuated from their homes, temporarily. They might leave immediately and live in any hotel, motel, or apartment they chose. The costs would be paid by the Federal Disaster Assistance Administration. She continued to read and I repeated it; but nothing else she said made any differ-ence. They met our deadline and the Love Canal people were out! That's all that counted. Everyone was hugging me. TV and news-paper people were congratulating us. I needed to find Marie and share this moment with her.

Someone brought a case of champagne. Corks were popping. We were so happy. People were laughing, crying, hugging each other, dancing around, and saying: "We won! We won! We're out!"

Although it was only to be a temporary move, we knew that if they moved us temporarily, we would eventually be moved permanently. I finally found Marie and poured a bottle of champagne over her head. It was a wonderful day, with more happy people than I had seen in the past two years. The office filled with flowers, fruit baskets, and other gifts, from people congratulating us on our victory.

We celebrated by taking the red carnations we had been wearing since taking the hostages and throwing them into the air, saying we were now free! Our babies would be safe from further exposure to Love Canal poisons.

5

STILL
STUDYING
THE PROBLEM

The association office was very busy after residents moved into area hotels, motels, and apartments. People were in and out, calling on the phone, telling us where they moved and giving us their new phone numbers. Of course, the temporary moves created a host of problems: "How do I get my children to school every day? I have no car, and the buses don't come through this way." "The restaurant closes at 9:00 and my husband doesn't get home from work until midnight. I have no stove in the hotel room. How do I feed him?" "My daughter has a learning disability. She can't adjust to all the change. The doctors said she needs a familiar routine. What do I do?" And of course reporters were everywhere looking for a story, looking for an angle.

Phil Donahue and Political Action

The Phil Donahue Show called. They wanted us to appear on their June 18 show. The reaction in the office was different this time, compared to the show in October 1978. In October, everone was excited. "Phil Donahue—wow!" Now, residents reacted differently. "Donahue. That's great press. Now we'll get the politicians to move!" It was exciting the first time because it was

Phil Donahue. Everyone loves Phil. Now our people looked at the show as a tool to use in pushing the government to relocate us permanently. By this time we understood how politicians react to public pressure, how to play the political game. We eagerly agreed to go, and found forty other residents to go with us. Donahue paid all of our expenses. The mayor of Niagara Falls, who had not been invited, insisted that he appear on the show.

With the presidential election coming up that fall, politics was on everyone's mind. Politicians who had helped us in the past two years knew we understood and appreciated their efforts. But others whom we had never heard of, who never so much as called our office to offer support, were calling us, telling us all they would do to help if we supported them. We quickly let them know we knew the game. But it was a political year and in the past, we won major victories during the campaign for governor. By learning from our previous experience, we knew we could exert considerable pressure before the presidential election.

We began raising money to go to the Democratic Convention to demonstrate our plight.

Excitement ran high among the residents who were to appear on the Phil Donahue Show. Women had their hair done, men had their best suits sent out to be cleaned. Forty people were to be bused to Chicago, a ten-hour ride. Debbie Cerrillo was in charge of coordinating the bus trip.

The mayor and I flew down the night before. I wanted to take the bus with my friends, but I had too much work to be done. I couldn't afford the time on the bus.

Coincidentally, we all arrived at the hotel at the same time, all except the mayor. I don't know where he stayed. The hotel lobby was total confusion. Many of the rooms were not ready. Some residents were trying to get their rooms changed. One couple's room had no bed. When they were given a different room, it was full of garbage—beer bottles and papers—and the sheets hadn't been changed. Another couple went to their room, but the window had no windowpane. When they called the front desk to tell them the window was missing, the clerk told them to look behind the curtain, that the windows slid behind one another. The resident explained she had looked, and said that it was gone! The clerk asked the woman what she did with it.

By late that evening everyone was settled. I passed the word for everyone to meet in the bar at 9:00.

At 9:00, we took over the bar. Everyone was tired but too

excited to sit still long. I stood on a chair to get everyone's attention, something that had become a habit since Love Canal began.

I told everyone when to meet in the morning and to bring
their luggage because we wouldn't be coming back. We then
planned how we would handle the Phil Donahue Show. We
wanted to show the world the kind of mayor we had, how he was
more interested in tourism than in saving our lives. But we
shouldn't spend more than a few minutes on that issue even if Phil
wanted to. We had to get the *real* issues across. Each resident was
assigned an issue. One told of the chromosome tests. Another
was to concentrate on her multiple miscarriages. Another was to
ask for telegrams from across the country to the White House—in
support of permanent relocation. I coached them to get their
point in, no matter the question asked. For example, if Donahue
asked what you thought of the mayor, and your assignment was to
discuss miscarriages, you should answer: 'I don't like the mayor
because I have had three miscarriages and other health problems,
and he won't help us. Or; "My family is sick, and the mayor
won't help us. That's why we need people to send telegrams to
the White House for permanent relocation. Maybe the White
House will help us." And so on.

The next morning, our bus took us to the studio. The
Donahue staff was great! They had a huge breakfast ready in a
beautiful dining room.

The mayor and I were hooked up directly to microphones.
The residents had one to pass around. The residents were great!
Each and every one followed through with our plan. An outside
caller was also helpful. He wanted to lock up local, state, and
federal authorities. Although the residents were hard on the
mayor, they didn't dwell on him. Phil took care of him in two
statements. He said our mayor reminded him of the mayor in
Jaws. What if people were being eaten by sharks? "We need to
keep the beaches open. We need the tourist trade."

After the show, we received thousands of letters and telegrams of support, and a great many people wrote to the White
House. That was truly helpful. I have heard that politicians
count letters and then multiply by fifty to estimate public support
on an issue.

In July, I went on a speaking tour of California arranged by
Jane Fonda and Tom Hayden. I visited many sites with problems
similar to ours. I was able to give advice, based on our experiences.
I told the leaders of each community that it wasn't hopeless, that

they could win. "Stick with it. We are!"

I got letters of support from the city councils of Los Angeles and San Francisco and from many organizations and individuals. Through some friends, I raised enough money to pay for a bus to take us to the Democratic Convention. It was a successful trip, and I was pleased with the results.

The Love Canal Boat People

We received the money from California in time to rent a bus to go to New York City for the Democratic Convention.

Many residents came in to the office to make signs and posters. We needed something different, something unique. Hundreds of people would be there pressing their causes. We wanted something that would stand out from the rest. We knew it was vital to get media attention in order to apply political pressure.

Because there had been so much talk about the Cuban refugee "boat people," we decided that would be our theme. We made signs calling ourselves the LOVE CANAL BOAT PEOPLE. Since President Carter recognized and helped those who came to him on boats, perhaps he would help us. We bought toy rubber rafts and wrote CARTER'S BOAT PEOPLE all over them.

We left Niagara Falls about eleven that evening. Most of the people slept on the eight-hour bus ride to New York City. We arrived early in the morning and were able to pick a strategic location where we would be seen.

We set up in our designated place and walked around holding our boats up, chanting, "President Carter, hear our plea. Set the Love Canal people free! 2-4-6-8—Help us now before it's too late!" Because we arrived early, we received good coverage. There wasn't a lot of competition for media attention. We walked all day!

Many residents who had never been exposed to New York City were surprised and amused by the people of New York. A little old man with green hair and beard came up and talked to us. The residents became more nervous when a large group came down the street talking and yelling. "President Carter is a liar! We're going to set his ass on fire." The police stopped the group before they reached us, but many of the residents wanted to leave. Although the protest was successful in gaining media attention, it distressed me to see my friends and neighbors lying down on their rubber boats exhausted. Some of the senior citizens didn't feel as if they had the energy to walk two blocks to our bus. One said, "I'm going to be sixty-five soon, and I feel like eighty. My whole body hurts. Lois, you may have to help me to the bus." He said it with a smile, but I knew he meant it. He, like most of the families, had unwavering courage. The residents were willing to do anything to achieve permanent relocation. This man wanted to live where it would be safe for his grandchildren to visit him again.

By now the Revitalization Committee had been established. We were waiting for federal funds necessary to match state funds to purchase our homes. Senator Javits' bill had passed the House and the Senate. The bill gave the President authority to purchase Love Canal homes. Now we had to wait and see if President Carter would sign it.

In mid-September I received a call from ABC's *Good Morning America.* They wanted me on their show. This was just what we needed: national coverage close to election time. But the people in the office weren't excited when I told them I was going on the show. They were tired and frustrated. Living in the hotels with all their uncertainties had drained them.

I knew the significance of this show at this particular time and was excited and eager because of the opportunity. I arranged for my mother to watch the kids, ironed something to wear, and caught the plane for New York City. Mike Cuddy, New York State's on-site coordinator, went on the show with me. I met him at the Buffalo airport.

ABC put us up in a lovely hotel and sent a limousine to drive us around. I enjoyed the VIP treatment. It made me feel special. Once in the studio, I met Dave Hartman for the first time. He was pleasant and friendly and made me feel as if I knew him for years. I felt comfortable with him.

This time I had enough time to say what I needed to say in order to push the Carter administration into doing something. I described the health effects, the present hotel living arrangements, and how people were suffering. Some marriages had broken up, and children were becoming insecure. I accused the EPA's Barbara Blum, the White House, and the Carter Administration of washing their hands of the Love Canal issue. It worked. The show aired September 19. On September 30 I received a phone call that President Carter was coming to Niagara Falls. He wanted me to be

present when he signed the agreement with the State of New York
appropriating $15 million to purchase all the homes. —Thank
God!

The President's Visit

Because the President was coming, I believe someone was outside
my apartment all night and I think my phone was tapped. I spent
most of the night trying to figure out what I would do. The next
morning, I showered and went to the office. Everyone was
making signs. I told them to keep them clean, because we need
something from President Carter. We don't want to alienate him.
One of the women who worked in the office asked me if I were
going to see the President in jeans, messy hair, and bare feet?
That's the way I often dressed around the office. If she were
going to see the President, she would be home all day fixing her
hair and getting ready. She was so nervous; it was as if she were
going to meet the President.

I went home late that afternoon. Debbie Cerrillo came over
with a gift for President Carter, a Love Canal T-shirt with a huge
blue ribbon. Today was President Carter's birthday. I didn't
think they would let me give it to him, but I thought I'd try. It
was a great idea.

I curled my hair, put on a dress, and put a white flower in
my hair to signify the freedom of Love Canal hostages and support
for the American hostages in Iran (many public figures had been
wearing white carnations to show support for our people in Iran).

Most of the residents went to the airport. I went to the
Niagara Falls Convention Center where the President was to sign
the bill. Unfortunately, the security guard took the T-shirt and
wouldn't let me present it to the President. I had no idea of what
I was going to do, but, I learned, the President did not intend to
meet with me, only to sign the bill.

Reporters and cameras were everywhere. The invited guests
looked like a who's who of government. Everyone wanted to
know what I would do. I just kept saying I would try my best to
talk to the President. Senator Javits came in. I went over to
thank him for getting the bill passed. I asked him if he could
introduce me to the President. He said he would do his best. I
was giving a news statement when President Carter came in.
Everyone stood up and applauded. When we sat down, I chose

an aisle seat. The Secret Service surrounded me. I felt like a criminal. People who knew me were watching to see what I would do. I felt awkward.

President Carter began his speech. I needed to tell the President that residents couldn't afford to buy homes at today's mortgage rates. We needed low-interest loans. I couldn't stand up and scream out that we wanted more. We would lose all public sympathy. Then I heard President Carter mention the association and my name. Everyone was looking at me now. I thought: *Great. My mother will love it!* I was looking for an opportunity to talk to the President. President Carter and Governor Carey sat down at the table on stage to sign the agreement. Everyone in the audience sat quietly in their seats. It was my last chance to do something—but what?

I stood up and stepped out in the aisle. The President and the Governor were directly in front of me. Still not knowing what to do, I slowly walked to the front. A rope was strung across the stage about a foot from the platform. Governor Carey began to speak. I stood in the center of the aisle, with my hands folded in front of me, staring up into President Carter's eyes. Javits whispered to Carter, and the President invited me up to the stage in the middle of Carey's speech. The cameras clicked and flashed. I thought how annoyed Carey must be with Carter and me interrupting his speech. I was surprised but I was surprisingly calm. Once on stage, I looked out over the audience and saw some of the residents from other groups, residents who had said I wouldn't get to see the President. I caught the eye of one woman who annoyed me a great deal and smiled prettily at her. As Jackie Gleason used to say, "How *sweet* it is!"

Then I got down to business. I thanked President Carter for the $15 million and I told him I brought him a birthday present (as a peace offering). I went on to say I had been trying to meet with him for two years. I explained our problems and asked him for low-interest mortgage money similar to that available to victims of floods and hurricanes. It wasn't easy to carry on a conversation on the stage, but I persisted. We spoke about the Superfund legislation as well. I was surprised at how well versed he was. It was not the best place for a conversation, but I was able to lobby with him for about twenty minutes. Even though my mouth didn't stop for the twenty minutes, some strange ideas went through my head. Every time Carter held my hand or put his arm around me, I thought: *Boy, that's a good political move. America will love it.* It was silly; I was thinking of politics rather than enjoying the moment.

Carter didn't talk much. He had to address whoever went up to the microphone and smile, shake his head, and periodically chuckle. He was much smaller than I imagined, only two or three inches taller than I. I didn't think his teeth were as large as the cartoons made them out to be.

After the ceremony, everyone rushed out. I had forgotten my purse and went back to get it. That gave me an opportunity to talk to Congressman LaFalce and Senator Javits. I told them I had discussed interest rates and mortgage money and asked them to follow through. Both agreed to talk to President Carter on the trip back to Washington. I knew they would do what they could.

Later, I picked up the kids and went home. My mother had been trying to get me for hours. She was so proud that her little girl had been commended by the President and had stood on the stage next to him. She wanted to know every detail; she was so happy. She had been at my side throughout this Love Canal craziness; in her mind, this made it all worthwhile. She bought dozens of copies of the paper and mailed the pictures to every one she knew. After talking with her awhile, I began to feel the excitement. I had stood with the President of the United States! After two years of trying to see him, I had finally met and talked with him. It wasn't the best of circumstances, but how many people get to talk directly to the President for twenty minutes! I felt a real sense of satisfaction, once I had time to think about it, but it wasn't *my* success. It was the association's!

The Revitalization Committee

By February 1981, over 400 families had moved from Love Canal, never to return. Hundreds more were building or looking for homes or preparing to move to apartments. Some families may decide to continue living at Love Canal. Most of those do not have small children, and by the terms of the agreement between New York State and Washington, they have three years in which to decide.

The Revitalization Committee was given $20 million to buy homes, assist renters in their moves, and revitalize the neighborhood. The agreement between the state and the federal government gave New York State $7.5 million in a grant and $7.5 million

Hundreds of people flocked to a meeting held by state
officials in hopes of finding some answers. *Courtesy
Niagara Gazette, photo by Andrew J. Susty*

as a loan. The state hoped to regain the loan from its lawsuit against Hooker Chemical. The $15 million went to the local Revitalization Committee.

The committee, once residents move, intends to revitalize the community by offering homesteads or giving tax breaks, or by making low-interest home-improvement loans as incentives. President Carter signed the bill because of residents' mental anguish, not because federal officials agreed there was a health problem at Love Canal. New York's commissioner of health admitted that there were hazards for pregnant women and small children, but he has not said Love Canal would be dangerous for others to live there! The Environmental Protection Agency collected air and soil samples during the fall of 1980, but they are still arguing about how to interpret the data. However, even the health department admits the sewers and creeks in the area are contaminated. The Center for Disease Control is supposed to conduct new health studies on residents and former residents of Love Canal. These studies are two years too late. Families that have moved from the canal have already seen dramatic changes in their health. People constantly tell me how well their children and they feel since leaving Love Canal.

Hooker continues to deny responsibility for Love Canal. Their public relations people are hard at work to change Hooker's image. They are defendants in lawsuits worth billions of dollars in clean-up costs, relocation, and property and health damages to the citizens of the area, and they want to sway public opinion. More important, industry wants to continue to bury its wastes in the ground—creating new Love Canals across the country, because it's more profitable than to dispose of the wastes safely.

The Love Canal People

The people of Love Canal are quite different now than they were two or three years ago. They no longer have blind faith in government. They now realize that government cannot be counted on to protect health, property, and well-being without a battle.

Many have come to hate government, because they have been hurt so badly, lied to so often, and treated so terribly. The Love Canal families are "good citizens" who pay their taxes on time and worry when they can't. They vote in every election. They are blue-collar, middle-class Americans. They mind their own business, keep their houses and property neat, and spend most of their time raising families.

Love Canal families have changed their values, their lifestyles, and their priorities. Parents sometimes panic when their child has a common cold. There's always a concern whether it is a cold or the beginning of something worse because their children were exposed to toxic chemicals. Underneath, they worry that chemicals will take a toll in their family in the form of cancer, birth defects, or some other illness. It's especially true among families who have had no special health problems. "When will it be our turn?" a woman asked one day.

Love Canal couples are reevaluating their lives. They are wondering if they really should have another child—or their first child—because of the high risk of stillborns, miscarriages, and birth defects. There are no medical tests available to identify whether a man or a woman has had damage to the reproductive system from chemical exposure. A woman has to become pregnant first, but even then tests are not 100-percent certain, and the only answer would be an abortion. Both men and women have matured as a result of this tragedy. They appreciate their spouses more. Our community was made up of families in which the man went to work and the woman stayed home and cared for the home and the children. You rarely saw husbands doing the laundry or cooking. But because of the canal crisis, the women did most of the work at the Homeowners Association. In the evening, the couple shared household tasks. Before, most of the men came and went as they pleased and the women stayed at home with the families and their hobbies. But because the women were active during the crisis, many found a new independence which they like. As a result, many women are now going to work or becoming involved in community organizations and in activities outside of their homes.

Unfortunately, in some cases, one family member grew and the other didn't. That sometimes caused marital problems, and in some cases, divorces. Some marriages at Love Canal ended in divorce because of the strains on the families throughout the crisis. Moving in and out of hotels and motels, sick children who just never seemed to get well, personal guilt for moving to *that* house, and the frustration and fear of being trapped. Husbands felt helpless trying to protect their families while wives continually cried because they feared something would happen to their babies.

The small children suffered the most. They did not understand *chemicals*, *dioxin*, or exactly how they might be harmed. Even though parents explained many times, the children couldn't understand what they couldn't see or touch but could sometimes smell. The odor around the canal was normal to the children. They could not comprehend exactly what their mothers were telling them. Many had nightmares imagining what "chemicals" looked like and then having an imaginary "thing" attack them. Many children lost their sense of security. Mom was not home as she used to be. Either dad or a baby-sitter was caring for them. Some of the children went to three different schools and had to keep adjusting and making new friends. Children who attended high school since ninth grade and wanted to graduate with their classes were pulled out of school in their junior or senior years because the family moved to a new home in a different district or a different state.

Families moved in and out of hotels several times. Small children had problems adjusting. Mom told them they couldn't bring their toys, that she would get new ones because the toys might be contaminated, or there were too many toys for the small hotel rooms. Children wanted to go home to their own rooms where things were familiar and have mom greet them at the door after school, back to their friends, their bikes, and their own small worlds.

From the beginning, signs of insecurity surfaced in many children. Some had behavioral problems in school. Some sucked their thumbs, wet their beds, had nightmares, or cried at every little thing. The total psychological damage to our children has not been measured, but it will stay with them for a long time. Many may need help in the future to cope with their problems.

The Love Canal Homeowners Association Will Go On

The Love Canal Homeowners Association will go on in some form. We have been successful. We fought "City Hall," and we won! The association brought a new awareness to the world of what can happen if toxic, hazardous wastes are buried in the earth—our earth, not industry's earth. We are searching for alternative methods for toxic waste disposal. There is new legislation to handle "Love Canals," the Superfund. Perhaps government officials will now try to use existing legislation to avoid Love Canals.

Communities are joining together to educate themselves and the public about the hazardous-waste issues. They are protesting, fighting new landfills proposed for their backyards, and fighting to clean up the existing dumps. I have been busy talking with people in communities, with government officials, with anyone who will listen, explaining what happened at Love Canal and how it can be avoided elsewhere.

Many of the communities I visited, in California, Rhode Island, Pennsylvania, and Massachusetts, are suffering as we were. Their children are sick. Their air, their soil, and their drinking water are contaminated, and their local and state governments are not properly investigating the problems or looking for solutions. In my visits to polluted communities, I try to offer advice about what we learned at Love Canal to help them organize more effectively. I explain how we organized our community, how we conducted a health survey, how to identify environmental contamination in their communities; what protests worked for us and how and when to use them; how to work with the media to educate the public and gain additional support. I am doing this because I feel a responsiblity to others faced with hazardous-waste problems. I know the fight they will face, and I can offer the sort of help no one else can. We have been through it all. It sickens me, but it also motivates me when I hear or see a child believed to be affected by toxic chemicals, sick with cancer, leukemia, or some other disease. It is unneccessary to sacrifice our children. They *can* be protected.

For these reasons, and more, we will be establishing a National Citizen's Clearinghouse for Hazardous Waste problems. We want to work directly with communities, individuals, and small municipalities to assist them at the local level, with information to fight industry and move government to resolve their problems. We are putting together data on toxic chemicals, on dangerous exposure levels, on health problems, and on safe disposal methods. We can assist in conducting health and other surveys to determine the extent of each community's problems. We can offer suggestions to organize local communities to speak with one strong voice. We are collecting information on existing laws for financial and other assistance and on how to identify an attorney who is knowledgeable about environmental issues. We are preparing lists of laboratories and physicians with experience in health damage related to chemical exposure. We can help local communities identify government agencies with responsibility for answering their quesions and concerns. I hope the clearinghouse will help people across the country to better understand and solve hazardous-waste problems.

Love Canal is not over. The families will suffer from Love Canal the rest of their lives. If the Revitalization Committee has its way, they will resell most of the homes to new, innocent victims. Five or ten years from now, you will probably hear the cries from people at Love Canal once again. The residents of Love Canal learned a lesson; I'm not sure that government and industry have. It will be up to us, as citizens, to tell them forcefully they can't cover over Love Canals. All our lives are at stake.